Unto Him Be Glory

- Why God's People Praise the Lord -

by

Bob Pitman

Unto Him Be Glory

ISBN: 978-0-9829875-1-3

Scripture quotations are from the King James Version of the Bible unless otherwise stated.

Printed in the United States of America

Dedication

This book is dedicated to

Vance and Brett Pitman,

My two sons, who have always been a joy to their parents and whose faithful walk with God has been a blessing. Both are godly pastors, Bible preachers, and loving husbands and fathers.

Table of Contents

Acknowledgements

Debbie Hargis, my former Administrative Assistant at
Kirby Woods Baptist Church in Memphis, TN, for her
gracious spirit, helpful suggestions, and unique gifts in
preparing and formatting this book.

Ken "Moose" Herrington, pastor of Salem Baptist
Church, Aynor, SC, for his insights in the
message entitled, "There is a Lad Here."

Junior Hill, "America's Beloved Evangelist,"
who inspired and encouraged me
to go into a writing ministry.

Preface

So much is said today about "Praise and Worship" you would think they had just been invented, but that is not true. God's people have always been involved in praising and worshipping the Lord. The present misconception is due to the fact that in today's church life, praise and worship have been identified with a certain style of music. Music is a wonderful tool that greatly enhances worship, but in and of itself, music is not worship. Great hymns of the faith and contemporary Christian music are both important in the experience of praise and worship, but they are not the essence of worship.

Worship is an attitude of the heart which understands the smallness of man and the greatness of God. That idea was expressed by David in Psalm 8:4, *"What is man, that thou art mindful of him? and the son of man, that thou visitest him?"* Genuine worship is an experience of loving God with the whole heart. We praise Him because of Who He is and what He has done. Hopefully, the messages in this book will encourage you to love Him more and give Him all the glory.

Evangelist Bob Pitman
Muscle Shoals, Alabama

Unto Him Be Glory

[20]Now unto him that is able to do exceeding abundantly above all that we ask or think, according to the power that worketh in us, [21]Unto him be glory in the church by Christ Jesus throughout all ages, world without end. Amen. (Ephesians 3:20-21)

Unto Him be glory! The word "glory" is used in at least four different ways in the New Testament. First, it refers to the PERSON of God. In John 1:1 we read, *"In the beginning was the Word, and the Word was with God, and the Word was God."* Then, in verse 14, John declares, *"And the Word was made flesh, and dwelt among us, (and we beheld his glory, the glory as of the only begotten of the Father,) full of grace and truth."* In that context, the word "glory" describes the very Person of God.

Second, the word "glory" is used to speak of the PRESENCE of God. Luke 2:8-9 states, *"And there were in the same country shepherds abiding in the field, keeping watch over their flock by night. And, lo, the angel of the Lord came upon them, and the glory of the Lord shone round about them: and they were sore afraid."* In this text the word "glory" refers to the brilliantly shining presence of the Lord that had so overwhelmed the shepherds they were terrified by it. In the Old Testament, this shining presence of the Lord was referred to as the *shekinah* glory of God.

Third, "glory" is used in Romans 8:18 to describe the PLACE where God dwells. Paul wrote, *"For I reckon that the sufferings of this present time are not worthy to be compared with the glory which shall be revealed in us."* The apostle is contrasting this present world in which we live with the future world in which we shall live. Today the children of God live on the earth, but tomorrow we shall live in Heaven. Earthly life is a life of suffering, but life in Heaven is a life of glory. I have an idea that when we enter Heaven, the first word that shall come out of our mouths will be "GLORY!" So the word "glory" describes the state of blessedness we shall experience when we go to live in the place where God dwells.

In Ephesians 3:21, however, the word "glory" does not refer to person, presence, or place. In this text it means PRAISE. The Greek word translated "glory" is *doxa*. It is the word from which we get the English word "doxology." From time to time in our churches we sing the Doxology. The very first word of the Doxology is "Praise." We sing, *"PRAISE God from Whom all blessings flow. PRAISE Him all creatures here below. PRAISE Him above ye heavenly hosts. PRAISE Father, Son, and Holy Ghost."*

There are three very important things to observe in this passage of Scripture: the **P**erson we praise, the **P**ower by which we praise Him, and the **P**lace in which we praise Him.

I. THE PERSON WE PRAISE

In Ephesians 3:20, Paul writes, "Now unto him." In verse 21, he says, "Unto him." The "him" about whom Paul writes is the Person we praise. Who is the "him" being described? The "him" we praise is GOD. The third chapter of Ephesians describes Him in several ways. In verse two, He is the God of grace. In verse three, He is the Revealer of mysteries. In verse seven, He is the Giver of gifts. In verse nine, He is the Author of creation. In verse ten, He is the God of wisdom. In verse eleven, He is the God of eternal purpose. In verse fourteen, He is the Father of the Lord Jesus Christ. In verse sixteen, He is the Provider of strength by the Spirit. In verse nineteen, He is the God Who fills with all fullness. The Person we praise is God.

God is Impeccable in His Character

3

We praise God because He is impeccable in His character. There are no flaws in Him. He is absolutely holy. In Him there is no darkness at all. God does not have a dark side. He does not have any dirty pages in His life. He is the holy God. One day an angel in Heaven describing the Person of God said, "Holy." Another angel said, "That's not enough. "He is Holy, Holy." A third angel declared, "More! More! He is a thrice holy God! He is Holy, Holy, Holy."

When you read Isaiah 6:1-3, you discover the result of that angelic conversation. Isaiah states, *"In the year that king Uzziah died I saw also the Lord sitting upon a throne, high and lifted up, and his train filled the temple. Above it stood the seraphims: each one had six wings: with twain he covered his face, and with twain he covered his feet, and with twain he did fly. And one cried unto another, and said, Holy, holy, holy, is the Lord of hosts; the whole earth is full of his glory."* You can bring your microscopes of scrutiny and examine Him for all eternity, and you will find no fault in Him. Our God is impeccable in His character.

God is Immutable in His Disposition

Let me tell you a second reason why we should praise God. He is immutable in His disposition. The word "immutable" means unchangeable. The Bible informs us that God does not ever change. He declared, *"For I am the LORD and I change not"* (Malachi 3:6). God never changes in His disposition. He is always loving. He is always righteous. He is always holy. He is always victorious. He is always majestic. He is always

4

glorious. He is always powerful. He never changes.

God does not have mood swings. God does not have imbalanced hormones. God is not a moody God. There are some people that you must walk around as though you are walking on eggshells. You never know what mood they may be in at any given moment. You may speak to them one day and they will say, "Why, hello there, brother. I'm glad to see you." You might speak to them another day and they will pour out their wrath on your head. Why? Because they are moody. They have mood swings. But beloved, God is not like that.

God is always the same. You could count on Him in the past. You can count on Him in the present. You can count on Him in the future. He never, never, never changes. The Psalmist said, *"even from everlasting to everlasting, thou art God"* (Psalm 90:2). That means you can stand at any point in history and look back as far as you can look, and look ahead as far as you can look, and God is always the same. What He always has been, He is now. What He is now, He always will be. He is immutable in His disposition.

God is Infallible in His Word

A third reason we should praise God is because He is infallible in His Word. God is a God Who cannot lie. Every word that God has ever spoken is absolutely true. The Bible which God has given to us is true. The Apostle Paul affirmed this when he declared, *"All scripture is given by inspiration of God, and is*

5

profitable for doctrine, for reproof, for correction, for instruction in righteousness: that the man of God may be perfect, thoroughly furnished unto all good works" (2 Timothy 3:16-17).

Jesus Christ is the Son of God. Jesus tells the truth and He is the truth. He is the express image of the Father. Some people tell untruths in error, by mistake, while others lie intentionally. In a world of hypocrisy, deceit, outright lying, and ignorant misinformation, it is refreshing to remember that God is infallible in His Word. That makes Him worthy of being praised.

God is Indestructible in His Authority

God in indestructible in His authority. This is a fourth reason to praise Him. He has all power. There are no earthly powers nor any powers in Hell which can topple the authority of God. God is not sitting in Heaven eating His fingernails wondering how things are going to turn out. He is not constantly calling the councils of Heaven together to find out how things are going in His creation. He is not troubled by the threats of terrorism. He is not unsettled by the utterances of the ungodly. He is not immobilized by the insults of infidels. He is not horrified by the howling of the heathen. The Psalmist settled the issue when he declared, *"Why do the heathen rage, and the people imagine a vain thing? The kings of the earth set themselves, and the rulers take counsel together, against the Lord, and against his anointed, saying, Let us break their bands asunder, and cast away their cords from us. He that sitteth in the heavens shall laugh: the*

Lord shall have them in derision" (Psalm 2:1-4).

God is Incomparable in His Ability

Not only should we praise God because He is impeccable in His character, immutable in His disposition, indestructible in His authority, and infallible in His word, we should praise Him because He is incomparable in His ability. In our text Paul states that God is ABLE! It is His ability that makes Him worthy of being praised. Beloved, our God is able.

Not only does the text tell us that God is able, it says, *"Now unto him that is able to do."* God is able TO DO. That's important. You see, there are a lot of folks who have ability that do not do anything. There are some folks who have the ability to sing, but they don't ever sing for the Lord. There are some folks who have the ability to give, but they don't give anything to the Lord. There are some folks who have the ability to teach, but they don't ever teach God's Word. There are some folks who have the ability to invite others to come, but they don't ever invite anybody to come to the Lord's house. It is one thing to have ability, but it is something else to have the ability to do. God is able TO DO.

Look again at our text. It says, *"Now unto him that is able to do ALL that we ask."* Now you think about that. It doesn't say He is able to do some of the things that we ask. It doesn't say that He is able to do most of the things that we ask. It says that He is able to do "all that we ask." There is no prayer too hard for

7

God to answer. Sometimes God says, "yes." Sometimes God says, "no." Sometimes God says, "wait." But our God is able to do all that we ask.

But look what else the text says. It says that God is able to do all that we ask or THINK. Just ponder that awhile. He's able to do all that we ask or think. What a mighty God we serve. You see, He knows the meditation of our hearts. Now there are times when we have public prayer. In every worship service, someone leads us in public prayer. Those prayers are said verbally. Those prayers are said in the presence of everyone in the congregation. They are also said in the presence of all the angels and demons who might be present in that service. That is why there are times we pray silently, with our mouths closed. Why? Because there are times we don't want the demons to know what we're saying.

You say, "Now wait a minute, Bro. Bob. I believe the devil and his demons can read a person's mind."

Who told you that? That is absolutely false. The devil cannot read your mind. He is not omniscient. Yes, he can read your body language. He can read your facial expressions. Can't you look at somebody and tell when they are mad? Can't you look at somebody and tell when they are happy? Can't you look at someone and tell when they are worried? Can't you look at someone and tell when they are sad? You do that by reading their body language. The devil can do that too. He can read your body language, but he cannot read your mind.

Yes, there are times when you pray that you don't want the devil to know what you are saying to the Lord. There is something burning in your heart. It may be a problem in your life, or a person about whom you are concerned. It may be a decision you are facing in which you desperately need the wisdom of the Lord. You want to share your burden with God, but it is none of the devil's business. So you pray a nonverbal prayer. It is a prayer of the heart, but not a prayer of the lips. Because God is "able to do all that we ask or think," He can hear and answer even those kinds of prayers.

But our text does not stop there. It says, "He is able to do ABOVE all that we ask or think." Isn't that amazing? He is able to do above all that we ask or think. Well, what could possibly be above all that we ask or think? I don't know, but I do know that He is able to take care of it. Amen!

Look what else our text declares. It says, He is able to do ABUNDANTLY above all that we ask or think. The word "abundantly" means *beyond measure*. There are no limits in God's ability. The little boy said, "It just gets dooder and dooder and dooder." And he's right.

But it doesn't even stop there. Paul said, "Unto him that is able to do EXCEEDING abundantly above all that we ask or think." "Exceeding" means *more than*. God has the ability to do more than beyond measure. Imagine that! What is the Holy Spirit of God

doing here? He is purposefully adding clause after
clause to emphasize the ability of God. In a football
game, the Holy Ghost would have a penalty flag thrown
against Him for "piling on." This is not accidental, but
deliberate. The Holy Spirit wants us to know that God
is incomparable in His ability.

Beloved, God is worthy of our praise. He is
worthy because He is impeccable in His character,
immutable in His disposition, infallible in His Word,
indestructible in His authority, and incomparable in His
ability. That is the Person we praise.

II. THE POWER BY WHICH
WE PRAISE HIM

Notice, please, a second truth. Not only does
this text identify Person we praise; it identifies the
power by which we praise Him. Look again at
Ephesians 3:20. It says, "Now unto him that is able to
do exceeding abundantly above all that we ask or think,
ACCORDING TO THE POWER THAT WORKETH
IN US."

What is the power that worketh in us? That
power is the Holy Spirit of God. You might ask, "Bro.
Bob, who is the Holy Spirit?" Boy, I'm so glad you
asked that question! I want to settle once and for all
Who the Holy Spirit is. The Holy Spirit is the
indwelling presence of Christ in your life. That's why
verse 21 says, "Unto him be glory in the church BY
CHRIST JESUS." Verse 20 says, "According to the
power that works in us." Verse 21 says, "by Christ

Jesus." The Holy Spirit of God is the indwelling presence of Christ in your life. That's why the book of Romans proclaims, *"Now if any man have not the Spirit of Christ, he is none of his"* (Romans 8:9).

As Christians we profess that Jesus Christ lives in us. We joyfully sing, "You ask me how I know he lives? He lives within my heart." How does Jesus live in us? Does He live in us physically? I'm a pretty big fellow. If you were to cut me apart and take out all my bones and internal organs, I guess Jesus Christ could fit inside my skin. But if Christ lives in us physically, how is He going to fit into the body of a little boy or a little girl? It just doesn't make sense, does it?

Jesus does not live in us physically, but He lives in us spiritually. He lives in us by the Holy Spirit. Jesus lives in your heart and in mine by the Holy Spirit of God. The Holy Spirit is the indwelling presence of Christ in your life.

Many Christians are terrified by the doctrine of the Holy Spirit. They have been told that the Holy Spirit makes people do weird, maniacal things. But that is not true. Let me share with you some things every Christian should know about the Holy Spirit.

First, He convicted you of sin before you were saved. You may have known that some things were right and some things were wrong. You may have even been aware of some things that you had done that were wrong. But it was not until the Holy Spirit brought conviction in your heart that you saw yourself as a sinner before God and in desperate need of salvation.

11

Second, it was the Holy Spirit Who birthed you into the family of God. In the third chapter of the Gospel of John, we are told about a man named Nicodemus. He was a man of the Pharisees and a ruler of the Jews. He came to Jesus by night, so as not to be seen by other Pharisees. He attempted to flatter Jesus. He said, "Master, we know that you have been sent by God because no one could do the things you are doing unless God was with him." This was nothing more than an attempt to flatter the Lord Jesus. Jesus was not very fond of flattery. He did not often give it out, and He rarely received it from someone else.

Jesus interrupted Nicodemus in the middle of his flattering words and declared, "You must be born again!" Nicodemus was perplexed and queried "How can I be born again? Am I to reverse the biological clock and once again become an infant and re-enter the body of my mother?" Jesus instructed him that it was not a physical birth that was needed, but a spiritual birth. He needed to be born of the Spirit. When you trusted Jesus, that's what happened to you. You were born again by the Holy Spirit of God. He birthed you into the family of God.

Third, the Holy Spirit also is the One Who baptizes you into the body of Christ. The Apostle Paul stated, *"For by one Spirit are we all baptized into one body, whether we be Jews or Gentiles, whether we be bond or free; and have been all made to drink into one Spirit"* (1 Corinthians 12:13). It is the Holy Spirit of God Who baptizes every believer into the body of

Christ. The baptism of the Holy Spirit is not experiential. It has nothing to do with speaking in tongues. It has nothing to do with seeing visions. It has nothing to do with laughter or tears. The baptism of the Holy Spirit is positional. We assume our position in Christ as a result of the baptizing work of the Holy Spirit. That takes place in the life of every Christian at the moment of salvation.

Fourth, the Holy Spirit equips us to do the work of God. What do you think the purpose of spiritual gifts is? Do you think that the Holy Spirit of God gave you a spiritual gift so that you can just sit around and feel good about yourself? Do you think the Holy Spirit of God gave you a spiritual gift so you can brag about it to other people? That's what they were doing at the church in Corinth. There were some in Corinth who had the gift of tongues, and they felt that their gift was superior to all other spiritual gifts. Paul refuted that idea in the fourteenth chapter of First Corinthians. Why did the Holy Spirit of God give us spiritual gifts? He gave us spiritual gifts to equip us to do the work of God.

Fifth, the Holy Spirit also guides us into all truth. He is the author of the Bible, and every time you read it you are in the presence of the author. He longs to teach you God's Word. Education is a wonderful thing and knowledge of the Greek and Hebrew languages is admirable, but the Holy Spirit will guide any sincere saint who seeks to know the truth of Scripture.

Sixth, the Holy Spirit comforts you in times of trouble. He encourages you, He lifts you up, and He blesses you. That's why Jesus called Him the Comforter. When it seems like the world is caving in, all hope is gone, and the enemy is winning, there comes that sweet, blessed assurance of the Holy Spirit. He assures you that God is still in charge, and that He will work all things out according to His purposes.

Seventh, the Holy Spirit also intercedes for us when we don't know how to pray. Oh, there are times when we simply don't know how to pray, but there is never a time when the Holy Spirit doesn't know how to pray. Romans 8:26 affirms, *"Likewise the Spirit also helpeth our infirmities: for we know not what we should pray for as we ought: but the Spirit itself maketh intercession for us with groanings which cannot be uttered."* Sometimes we don't know how to pray, and He groans on our behalf. He intercedes for us.

Many times in my life I did not know how to pray. When I was a pastor, there were times I went into a hospital room and there would be someone there eaten up with cancer, and the family members were there as well. I knew the family members wanted me to pray that God would heal this person. But as I looked into the eyes of the person lying on the bed, I knew they wanted me to ask God to take them to Heaven. So how do you pray? Do you pray to please the one dying, or do you pray to please the ones standing there watching them die?

Thankfully, in those times when you just don't know how to pray, the Holy Spirit intercedes on your behalf. Isn't that good? He convicts us of our sin. He births us into the kingdom of God. He baptizes us into the body of Christ. He equips us for the work of the ministry. He comforts us when we're discouraged. He guides us into all truth, and He prays for us when we don't know how to pray.

But this passage in Ephesians 3 tells us an eighth thing the Holy Spirit does for us. He empowers us to praise God. "Now unto him that is able to do exceeding abundantly above all that we ask or think according to THE POWER THAT WORKETH IN US, unto him be glory in the church by Christ Jesus." The Holy Spirit of Jesus living inside of you will empower you to praise God, even when you do not feel like praising Him.

Beloved, anybody can praise God when things are going well. Anybody can praise God when all your loved ones are well. Anybody can praise God when you have enough money to pay all your bills. Anybody can praise God when all your children are doing as they should. But if you get a word from the doctor that you never wanted to hear, or if your children are breaking your heart and going astray, or if you have absolutely more month than you have money and you can still praise God, that's the Holy Spirit of God inside of you empowering you to praise Him.

This thing of praise is not just manufacturing an attitude. This thing of praise is not just raising of hands, though that's good to do. This thing of praise is not a matter of songs. Today we often hear, "Finally the church is singing praise and worship songs." What do you think we've been doing all these years? God's people have always praised Him and worshipped Him with our singing. Praise has nothing to do with the style of music you use. Praise is a matter of the heart when it is set on fire by the Holy Spirit of God.

III. THE PLACE IN WHICH WE PRAISE HIM

Notice the third great truth in this text. Paul declares, "UNTO HIM BE GLORY IN THE CHURCH." Now don't misunderstand. A Christian can praise God anywhere, at any time, under any circumstance. You can praise Him by yourself. You can praise Him in the car. You can praise Him in your bedroom. You can praise Him in your home at a family altar. You can gather as a family and read the Bible and have prayer and sing and praise the Lord. You can do that. But may I say to you, the most obvious and the most natural place where God ought to be praised is in the church.

I am not interested in being a part of the church that does not want to praise the Lord. Strange things are happening in some churches today. Some churches are more passionate about putting folks out of the church than they are about getting folks into the church. There are some churches that are spending more time explaining why God will not save certain people than they are trying to tell somebody how to get saved. I am not interested in being in that kind of a church. I want to be in a church where the Bible is preached, the Holy

Spirit of God brings conviction, people walk the aisle and give their lives to Jesus, and the church praises God for it. The church ought to be the house of praise to the Lord. When you go into God's house, there ought to be an attitude of praise. Never say, "I've got to go to church," but instead say, "I get to go to church, and I'm going to praise God while I'm there." Beloved, I do not go to church to find out about a football team, or the weather, or to see what someone is wearing. I go to praise God!

What do you think we're going to do in Heaven? In the fourth chapter of the Book of Revelation, verses ten and eleven, we read, *"The four and twenty elders* (which represent all the Old Testament and New Testament saints) *fall down before him that sat on the throne, and worship him that liveth forever and ever, and cast their crowns before the throne saying, Thou art worthy, O Lord, to receive glory and honour and power: for thou hast created all things, and for thy pleasure they are and were created."* That is PRAISE!

In the fifth chapter, verse five, Jesus Christ, the Lion of the tribe of Judah, the Root of David, the Lamb of God, has prevailed. He has taken possession of the sealed book and broken the seals. He is the Lord of Lords! Verses eight and nine tell us that the four and twenty elders fall down before the Lamb and they sing a new song unto the Lord. The words they sing are *"Thou art worthy to take the book, and to open the seals thereof: for thou wast slain, and hast redeemed us to God by thy blood out of every kindred, and tongue,*

17

and people, and nation: And hast made us unto our God kings and priests: and we shall reign on the earth." That is PRAISE! Again, in verse twelve, we see, *"Saying with a loud voice, Worthy is the Lamb that was slain to receive power, and riches, and wisdom, and strength, and honour, and glory, and blessing."* That is PRAISE! Then in verse fourteen, the saints of God in Heaven fall down and worship *"him that liveth FOREVER and EVER."* Friend, that is PRAISE and that is what we will do in Heaven!

We praise Him now in local churches around the world, but one day we will praise Him in the church triumphant when we get on the other side. That is why the Apostle Paul said in Ephesians 3:21, *"Unto him be glory in the church by Jesus Christ THROUGHOUT ALL AGES, WORLD WITHOUT END."* Our praise of Him here is a dress rehearsal of our praise of Him over there. No wonder Paul closed the verse by saying AMEN!

Not all people praise the Lord. Some do not praise Him because they have never experienced the wonder of salvation. They have never repented of their sins and called on Jesus to save them. Some Christians do not praise Him either. Some are backslidden, some are too proud, some live in fear, and some are even mad at God. Beloved, life is too short, and God is too worthy for us not to praise Him. Praise is a matter of obedience. Psalm 150:6 says, *"Let everything that hath breath praise the Lord. Praise ye the Lord."* Are you breathing? Then get with it, my friend, praise Him!

Praise is also a matter of fellowship with the Lord. Psalm 22:3 reminds us, *"But thou art holy, O thou that inhabitest the praises of Israel."* The word "inhabitest" means *the place where someone lives or is at home.* God lives in the praises of His people. That is where He is always at home. If you are experiencing a brokenness in your fellowship with God, then start praising Him and the fellowship will be restored.

The old hymn was right when it said: *"Praise the Lord, praise the Lord, let the earth hear His voice; Praise the Lord, praise the Lord, let the people rejoice. O come to the Father through Jesus the Son, and give Him the glory great things He hath done."*

19

Unto Him Be Glory

A Funeral Possession That
Turned into a Parade

[11]And it came to pass the day after, that he went into a city called Nain; and many of his disciples went with him, and much people. [12]Now when he came nigh to the gate of the city, behold, there was a dead man carried out, the only son of his mother, and she was a widow: and much people of the city was with her. [13]And when the Lord saw her, he had compassion on her, and said unto her, "Weep not." [14]And he came and touched the bier: and they that bare him stood still. And he said, "Young man, I say unto thee, Arise!" [15]And he that was dead sat up, and began to speak. And he delivered him to his mother.

(Luke 7:11-15)

The New Testament records that during His earthly ministry Jesus raised three people from the dead. In the fifth chapter of Mark, Jesus raised the daughter of Jairus from the dead. Jairus is identified as a ruler of the synagogue. Most of the rulers of the synagogues had already shunned Jesus and were doing everything in their power to discredit Him. But Jairus had a special problem. His twelve-year-old daughter was dying. He had done everything an earthly parent could do for a child, but she was still dying. He put aside his personal dislike of Jesus and forgot all about political correctness in the eyes of his peers. In desperation he comes to Jesus, explains his situation, and asks the Lord to go home with him to heal his daughter. Jesus agrees to go with him.

As they go, a delegation comes from the home of Jairus and informs them that the child has died. Jesus tells Jairus not to be afraid, but to just keep on believing. Upon arrival at the house, Jesus goes into the bedchamber where the lifeless body of the little girl was lying on the bed. Eyes that once sparkled were now shut. Lips that once sang little songs are now sealed. Hands that had played with rag dolls and made mud pies are now motionless. Legs that once ran and danced are now stilled. She is dead. Jesus reaches down and takes her by the hand and says to her, "Arise." And that is just what she did. She arose.

In the eleventh chapter of John, Jesus raises

Lazarus from the dead. Lazarus was a personal friend of Jesus. He lived in Bethany with his two sisters, Mary and Martha. Jesus visited in their home many times, He was loved in that home and he loved being in that home. Jesus was over twenty miles away from Bethany when Lazarus became seriously ill. Mary and Martha sent a messenger to Jesus requesting that He come immediately to Bethany and heal their brother. Having delivered the message, the messenger returned to Mary and Martha and told them he had completed his task.

However, Jesus did not go immediately to Bethany. He remained where He was until He finished doing what he went there to do. When He finally arrived in Bethany, Lazarus was already dead and had been buried for four days. Mary and Martha are heartbroken and express their disappointment that Jesus had arrived too late. Jesus assures them that He is never too late, but He is always right on time. He reminds them that He is the resurrection and the life, and then off to the graveyard they go. Jesus orders the cemetery workers to roll the stone away from the entrance of the tomb and then shouts, "Lazarus, come forth." Immediately Lazarus comes walking out of the tomb, ALIVE!

Our text for this message identifies the third person Jesus raised from the dead. He is not mentioned by name, but he had lived in the city of Nain and was the only son of his widowed mother. We are not told how this young man died. His death may have been caused by an accident or it may have been the result of

23

foul play. Some illness may have brought his life to an end. Only one thing is sure, he was dead.

The scene opens with two processions. First, there is a procession of LIFE. Jesus is going into the city and He is accompanied by many of his disciples and "much people." This was a large procession, and Jesus is the center of attention. Everyone in this procession is there because in some way Jesus had touched their lives. This is a happy throng of people, and they are laughing and singing and enjoying being in the presence of Jesus.

At the same time there is a procession of DEATH coming out of the city. It, too, is a large procession, consisting of "much people." The center of attention is the dead body of a young man in an open casket being carried by pall bearers to the cemetery to be buried, probably beside his deceased father. There is no laughing or singing in this procession except for a possible funeral dirge. Following the casket is a heartbroken mother. She has made this trip to the graveyard before when her husband died. Now she is making the trip once again to bury away the only other man in her life, her only son.

These two processions, the procession of life and the procession of death, meet head on at the city gate. What is Jesus going to do? I was raised in North Alabama. It is the custom there for all traffic to come to a stop when a funeral procession is approaching. You remain stopped and do not proceed until the funeral procession has passed by. You do not have to know the people in the funeral procession. It makes no difference what the color of their skin may be. All that matters is here is a family which is going through a hard time, and out of respect for them you pull over and let them pass. So what is Jesus going to do? Is He going to stop His procession and instruct the people in it to be quiet? Is He going to yield to the procession of death? NO! He does not stop, and He does not yield. Instead, He interrupts the funeral procession. He walks right over to the open casket and places His hands on its side. The pall bearers are shocked and immediately freeze in place. No one has ever seen anything like this. Jesus did three things.

I. HE REMOVED THE TEARS

Jesus looks at the boy's mother. She is sobbing beyond control. She has wept until her entire body is aching. Then Jesus issues a command to her. He says, "Weep not." It is not a request. It really is a command. He orders her to stop crying. If any preacher dared to do that at a funeral service, he would be fired from his pulpit. He would be called mean-spirited, cruel and heartless. But that's exactly what Jesus did. He can do it because He is going to fix the problem that has produced the tears.

In my ministry, which now extends over fifty-six years, there were many times when I walked into heart-breaking situations and my first thought was, "I wish I could fix it." But I never could fix it. Jesus, however, is a Master at fixing things. Nothing is too hard for Him. He is God in the flesh. He is Absolute

25

Master and Sovereign Lord.

Life is a vale of tears. There are tears of disappointment, tears of disease, and tears of death. Sometimes things do not turn out the way we planned. A seemingly happy marriage ends up in divorce, and tears of disappointment flow. Some of you reading this book have loved ones suffering from cancer or Alzheimer's, and the tears of disease often flow. When beloved members of our families pass away, the tears of death flow. The tears are real and the older a person gets the more they seem to flow.

In Psalm 56:8, God reminds us that He has a tear bottle. I'm not sure of all that means, but at least it means that our tears do not go unnoticed by the Lord. The tears of God's people do not drop into the dust and evaporate into nothingness. When followers of Jesus weep, their tears mysteriously and miraculously end up in God's tear bottle.

Warren Wiersbe was one of the greatest Bible preachers and teachers of the past sixty years. He said every preacher should have a Holy Spirit enlivened imagination. In my imagination, I look into the future and see the first time all of God's children gather together. Every Old Testament believer, every New Testament saint, and every person who has come to faith in Christ since the New Testament era ended gathered for the first time in the presence of God. In my imagination, I see God hold up that massive bottle and hear Him say, "Children of mine, these are the tears you shed while you lived on the earth." Then, in my imagination, I see Him throw that bottle as far as He can throw anything. As that bottle sails through the corridors of eternity, I hear God say, "Bye-bye tears. There are no tears in Heaven." He removed the tears.

II. HE RAISED THE BOY

Next, Jesus raises the boy from the dead. Looking into the face of the dead boy, He says, "Young man, I say unto thee, arise." Notice, he said, I SAY UNTO THEE. The absolute authority of Jesus is beyond question or challenge. He did not have to get the approval or permission of anyone to perform this miracle. He did not have to petition the Supreme Court, contact the White House, or even stand before the House Judiciary Committee. He acted on His own authority. He declared, "I SAY UNTO THEE." Beloved, Jesus Christ is Lord. You do not have to make Him Lord nor crown Him Lord, He IS Lord. He is Lord over disappointment, disease, and death. He is Lord over demons and the devil himself.

When Jesus said "arise" the Bible states, "He that was dead sat up and began to speak." Friend, that will break up a good funeral. I don't care how much money has been invested in flowers or how sharply the pall bearers are dressed. If you go to a funeral service and the corpse sits up and begins to speak, the funeral is over. Death was reversed, the grave was robbed, sadness was replaced, and the devil was rebuked. What a mighty Savior is He!

III. HE REUNITED THE FAMILY

Verse fifteen says, "And he (Jesus) gave him (the raised boy) back to his mother." I wish I had been there to see that. There are some things in the Bible I am glad I wasn't there to see, but I would have liked to watch this scene at the city gate take place. I think this mother had a spell. I can see her jumping up and down and screaming to the top of her voice, "My boy is back! My boy is back!" Then she wraps her arms around that son and squeezes like only a mother can do. What a scene!

All of God's people are anticipating a coming day of resurrection and a time of family reunion. Many of you have loved ones who have already passed to the other side and are already with the Lord. A mother, a father, a son, a daughter, a brother, a sister—absent from the body, but present with the Lord. If you belong to Jesus, you will one day be with them again in Heaven.

People ask interesting questions about that future experience in Glory. Some wonder, "Will we know one another in Heaven?" We know one another down here, and I am sure we will have as much sense in Heaven as we have on earth. In 1 Corinthians 13:12, Paul tells us that in heaven we shall know as we are known. In part, that means we shall know without introduction. No one will walk around Heaven with us and introduce us to other people. Yes, we will know one another over there.

Some people often ask about the marriage

relationship in Heaven. Jesus Himself answered that question, *"For in the resurrection they neither marry, nor are given in marriage, but are as the angels of God in heaven"* (Matthew 22:20). That seems to bother some folks.

One lady came to the preacher and said, "If my husband is not going to be my husband in Heaven, I don't want to go." Then her husband came to the preacher and said, "If my wife is going to be my wife in Heaven, I don't want to go." Aren't you glad God has that figured out!

Dr. R.G. Lee, famed Baptist preacher, once told about a man who married a lady named Milly. In time she died, and the man later married her twin sister, Tilly. After several years she also passed away. When it came time for the man to die, he was asked where he would like to be buried. He said, "Bury me right between Milly and Tilly, but tilt me a little towards Tilly." God has taken care of all that. Just understand, in Heaven no one will be lonely, and everyone will love everyone else perfectly.

When our text opened in verse eleven, there were two processions, life and death. However, by the end of verse fifteen, there was only one procession that remained, the procession of life. What happened? The procession of death had been swallowed up by the procession of life. That happens every time a person comes to faith in Christ. Jesus lifts you out of the procession of death and places you into the procession of life.

Which procession are you in today? Are you in the procession of life that leads to everlasting joy in Heaven, or are you in the procession of death that leads to everlasting sorrow in Hell? Jesus alone can take you out of death and put you into life. Then your funeral procession can become a parade!

~ 3 ~

There is a Lad Here

*¹After these things Jesus went over the sea of Galilee,
which is the sea of Tiberias. ²And a great multitude
followed him, because they saw his miracles which he
did on them that were diseased. ³And Jesus went up into
a mountain, and there he sat with his disciples. ⁴And the
Passover, a feast of the Jews, was nigh. ⁵When Jesus
then lifted up his eyes, and saw a great company come
unto him, he saith unto Philip, "Whence shall we buy
bread, that these may eat?" ⁶And this he said to prove
him: for knew he himself what he would do. ⁷Philip
answered him, "Two hundred pennyworth of bread is
not sufficient for them, that every one of them may take
a little." ⁸One of his disciples, Andrew, Simon Peter's
brother, saith unto him, "There is a lad here, which*

31

hath five barley loaves, and two small fishes: but what are they among so many?" [10]And Jesus said, "Make the men sit down." Now there was much grass in the place. So the men sat down, in number about five thousand. [11]And Jesus took the loaves; and when he had given thanks, he distributed to the disciples, and the disciples to them that were set down; and likewise of the fishes as much as they would. [12]When they were filled, he said unto his disciples, "Gather up the fragments that remain, that nothing be lost." [13]Therefore they gathered them together, and filled twelve baskets with the fragments of the five barley loaves, which remained over and above unto them that had eaten. (John 6:1-13)

When I was a teenager attending the Highland Baptist Church in Florence, Alabama, the young people had a thirty-minute private meeting with the pastor every Wednesday night before the churchwide prayer meeting service. I can still remember the night in 1965 when the pastor came into our meeting and introduced to us a brand-new gospel tract just released by Campus Crusade for Christ. It was called "The Four Spiritual Laws." It was a tool to be used for sharing the Gospel in order to win people to Christ, and since that time millions have been saved as a result of that wonderful soul-winning tract. It was the first Gospel tract I had ever seen, but it was not the first Gospel tract ever written. The Gospel of John was the first Gospel tract ever written.

There are thirty-seven specific miracles of Jesus recorded in the New Testament. John selected seven of those miracles and put them in his Gospel. He states his purpose for doing that in John 20:30-31, *"And many other signs* (miracles) *truly did Jesus in the presence of his disciples, which are not written in this book* (his Gospel): *But these are written, that ye might believe that Jesus is the Christ, the Son of God; and that believing ye might have life through his name."*

The seven miracles the Holy Spirit led John to select are as follows. In chapter two Jesus turns water into wine. In chapter four He heals the son of a nobleman at a distance of over twenty miles. In chapter five Jesus heals a man who had been paralyzed for thirty-eight years. In chapter six He miraculously feeds five thousand men, plus their wives and children, with five loaves and two fish. Also, in chapter six Jesus walks on water at the Sea of Galilee. In chapter nine He gives sight to a fully grown man who had been blind from birth. Finally, in chapter eleven Jesus raises Lazarus from the dead.

John tells us to behold these miracles, ponder them, look closely at them. Jesus did them. No one else did them, and no one else could have done them. Jesus is the Christ, and He is the Son of God. Believe in Him, commit your life to Him, and you will have everlasting life. Yes, the Gospel of John was the first Gospel tract ever written.

The focus of this sermon is the feeding of the five thousand. Of course, the five thousand was simply the number of the men. Most of them were married, and most of those married couples had children. There were easily more than twenty-five to thirty thousand who received the blessing of this miracle.

Of all the miracles of Jesus mentioned in the New Testament, this is the only one that is recorded in all four Gospels. Some of the miracles are recorded in three Gospels, some in two, and some only in one. But the feeding of the five thousand is the only one found in all four Gospels—Matthew, Mark, Luke and John. That should be an indication of its importance.

All four Gospels speak of the large crowd, the five loaves and two fish, and the twelve baskets full of leftovers when the eating was completed. But John mentions three things in his Gospel that are not mentioned in the other three Gospels. First, John inserts the names of Philip and Andrew into his account of the miracle. Matthew, Mark, and Luke do not mention any names at all. Second, John alone tells us the source of the loaves and fish. Andrew says, "There is a lad here." The lad is the one who had the loaves and fish. Third, John informs us that the loaves were *barley loaves* and the fish were *small fishes.* The other Gospel writers make no mention of the grain used in the bread or the size of the fish. These are not just meaningless facts, they are important to the message from this miracle.

On the morning that this miracle took place, Jesus and His disciples assembled on the northwestern shore of the Sea of Galilee beside the city of Capernaum. He gave His disciples a very specific assignment that would fill most of the day. He sent them out two by two to call the people to repentance. The people had turned their backs on God and they needed to repent. The disciples were not to preach any other message that day except repentance. After they completed their assignment, they were to come back and give Him a report concerning where they had been, what they had said, and the response of the people.

After the disciples were gone, Jesus began healing those around Him who were diseased and afflicted. As the day went on, the crowd got larger and larger. What probably began with less than a hundred people soon became a crowd numbering into the thousands. Finally, there were approximately thirty thousand in attendance, some being healed and the rest watching.

As the day began to come to a close the disciples return and give their report to Jesus. Jesus then instructs them to get in a boat there by the shore. Jesus gets in the boat with them, and they depart for the other side of the sea. They row over to the northeastern shore by the city of Bethsaida. It is only about a three-mile trip by water.

The multitude that had gathered throughout the day was not ready for their experiences with Jesus to be over. Have you ever been in a worship service in which the Spirit of God moved in such a mighty way that when the service was supposed to be over nobody wanted to go home? There was no need for more singing or preaching. People just wanted to stay around basking in the glory of God. That's the way it was with this crowd of thousands. As Jesus and His disciples row across the sea, this crowd starts walking around the northern shore. By land it was a distance of just over four miles.

Jesus and the disciples arrive at the other side of the sea first. They get out of the little boat and move up the side of the mountain. By the time the walking multitude gets there, the daylight is fading and the evening shadows are falling. When Jesus sees the approaching crowd, He is concerned that they be given their supper. The other Gospels tell us that the disciples recommended that Jesus send the crowds away, but Jesus would have none of that. He asks Philip where they could buy food to feed the multitude. Bethsaida was the hometown of Philip. He knew where the places to buy food were located, but Jesus was not asking where to buy food for information's sake. He was using this time to test Philip. Jesus already knew what He was going to do.

Philip had been following Jesus since the third day of Jesus' public ministry and had now been with Him for about two and a half years. Philip really loved Jesus, but still had areas in his life where he needed to grow. Philip informs the Lord that they only had about thirty to thirty-five dollars in their purse, and that was an insufficient amount to feed the crowd. Think about that. After two and a half years in public ministry, Jesus only had that meager amount of money in the till. He would have never made it as a modern televangelist living in mansions, flying self-owned airplanes, and amassing millions of dollars. Compared to that bunch, Jesus would have been considered a failure. But I'm sticking with Jesus! I wish that Philip would have responded, "Lord what we have is not sufficient, but YOU are," but he did not. Don't be too critical of Philip. Most Christians today have little understanding of the all-sufficiency of Christ.

Andrew then speaks. He had been following Jesus since the second day of His public ministry. Andrew was one of the first two followers of Jesus. Like Philip, Andrew was a genuine believer in the Lord. He really loved Jesus, but he, too, needed an expansion of faith. He introduces a little boy to Jesus and told him of the five loaves and two fish. Then he adds, "but what are they among so many." O, that he would have said, "Lord there are only five loaves and two fish here, but that is more than enough for YOU to feed the people," but he didn't. He, too, needed some spiritual growth in his life. Again, do not be too critical of Andrew. How is your faith? What are you believing God for today?

Now we come to the little boy. Since he is referred to as a lad, I assume he is somewhere between the age of seven and eleven. I can see him getting up early that morning. As he bounced out of his bedroom into the presence of his mother, he was ready for the day. Then I am sure his mother asked him the same question that mothers ask their sons today early in the morning, "Son, what are you going to do today?" He probably said, "I am going down to the seaside and see a man named Jesus. Mother, everybody is talking about him. They say he can walk on water, heal the sick and even raise people from the dead."

Then she asks, "How long are you going to be gone?" He says, "O Mother, I'm going to be gone all day long. I want to get as close to Him as I can get. I want to hear everything He says. Maybe I can even get close enough to touch Him."

Then her motherhood really kicks in. She says, "Well, if you are going to be gone all day you will need a little snack to eat when you get hungry." So she gets a little cloth sack and puts in five little biscuits and two small fish. When you read the word *loaves,* don't envision a loaf of bread like you would find in a grocery store. They were five little biscuits. She gives him the little sack and tells him to put it in his pocket. When he got hungry during the day, he could reach into that little sack in his pocket and nibble on the contents.

Then, off he goes, as fast as his little legs will take him, down to the seaside where Jesus was. All day long he watches Jesus as He heals the sick. He has never seen anything like it in his entire young life. He stands in amazement as he witnesses the blind seeing, the deaf hearing, and the lame walking. He is so absorbed in what he is seeing, it never occurs to him to reach into his pocket and get something to eat. He spends all day without ever getting hungry.

When Jesus and the disciples start across the Sea of Galilee and the crowd begins to walk around the northern shore, the lad joins in the march. He does not go home and ask his mother if he can go, he just goes. Sometimes it is simpler to get forgiveness than it is to get permission. Probably in that large crowd he has several uncles or aunts or cousins, so when the crowd begins to move, he just goes with the flow.

When they reach the other side, the little boy sees Jesus and His disciples on the hillside. I can see him running as fast as he can to get to Jesus. He gets as close as he can to the Lord, even within earshot. When he gets to where Jesus is, he overhears the conversation between Jesus and Philip concerning where to buy food. Jesus needs food, and for the first time that day the boy remembers what he has in his pocket. He then takes the little sack out of his pocket and shows it to Andrew, who in turn shows it to Jesus. Andrew probably chuckled as he peered into the bag and saw the contents. But Jesus did not laugh. He gave instructions for the men to be seated, then He blessed the little loaves and fishes.

After the blessing on the meal had been offered, it was time to serve the meal. The twelve disciples assemble before Jesus, each one with a large basket in his hands. Some people seem troubled about where the baskets came from. Who knows? Maybe they ran to Walmart and picked them up. One by one the disciples stand before Jesus as He breaks the bread and fish. Then the disciples distribute the food. Have you ever tried to feed thirty thousand people? It cannot be done with only twelve baskets of food. Each disciple came back again and again to have his basket filled. Every one of the disciples probably had to carry at least fifty baskets of food to feed a crowd that large. All the while Jesus stands in place breaking bread and fish with his hands—those wonderful, helping, healing hands.

Verse twelve says, *"When they were filled."* Did you see that? They were all filled. That means the whole crowd ate all they could hold. Philip had been concerned that there was not enough for everyone to have a little, but when Jesus stepped in they were all FILLED! What a Savior we serve! Jesus then instructs the disciples to gather the food that remained so that nothing be wasted, and each one of them returns with a full basket of leftovers. Jesus is more than enough. Hallelujah!

The little boy had seen the entire miracle unfold. He heard the blessing, he saw the baskets, he saw the food being served and eaten, and he saw the twelve baskets full of remaining food the disciples brought back to Jesus. What a day it had been for this lad! There are three things that are noteworthy about this boy.

I. HE DIDN'T HAVE MUCH

Do you remember what John told us about the loaves and fish that the other Gospel writers omitted? He said the loaves were barley loaves and the fish were small fishes. Barley was used to feed animals like cows, goats and horses, but was not used for human consumption. Barley was the poorest type of grain produced. The only people who ate barley were those who were impoverished, the poorest of the poor. The fish were about the size of the human palm. They had been split down the middle, gutted and dried in the sun. When you bit into them the texture would have been something like a thick potato chip. You see, he didn't have much.

Many Christians say they wish they could do more in their service of the Lord, but they think they don't have much to offer. Hey, it does not take much! Most Christians around the world do not have lots of money to give. Most of them could never sing a solo in church or even teach a Bible class. Sometimes the devil tries to intimidate those folks by telling them they are worthless and useless to God. But the devil is a liar and never to be believed. Every Christian is a child of God and important to Him. You do not have to be a scholar, or a great athlete, or an outstanding musician to effectively serve the Lord.

II. HE GAVE WHAT HE HAD

When this boy heard the Lord talking to Philip about the need for food, he had to make a decision. He thought, "He needs food; I've got food." So, he has to decide what to do. Is he going to give the five loaves and two fish to Jesus, or is he going to keep it? After all, it was his. His mother had prepared it for him to eat when he got hungry. Then, if he decides to give it to Jesus, he has to make another decision. Is he going to give all of it or only part of it? Without any hesitation, he gave it all.

It is a tragedy of modern Christianity that so many live their lives in fractions. They give a little to the Lord, but they keep back so much. That's not just true about money, it's also true about time and talents. We often sing, "I surrender all, I surrender all." Maybe, if we will get honest before the Lord, we ought to sing, "I surrender part from my selfish heart." Thankfully, this lad gave what he had.

III. JESUS USED WHAT HE GAVE

Jesus took what the boy gave and used it to bless the lives of thousands. Philip and Andrew did not pass their faith test that day, but this lad passed with flying colors. He believed that Jesus could take what he had and bring glory to Himself through it. That is real faith. Jesus will use you if you will give Him the opportunity. Just think how many lives could be blessed if you totally surrendered yourself to God. The people of this world desperately need to experience the blessing of God. Many are worshipping false gods that cannot bless anyone. Many others have twisted ideas about the God of the Bible and never see Him as a source of blessing. It just might be that you are the missing link. You may not have much, but if you will give it to God, He will use it for His glory to bless the lives of others.

Can't you see that little boy as the disciples serve all that food and then bring back twelve baskets full of leftovers? I see him with his eyes as big as saucers and his mouth wide open. Then, in my imagination, I hear him ask the Lord, "Jesus, where did all that come from?" Then I hear that remarkable voice of the Son of God reply, "It came out of your pocket."

Do you think that boy knew he had a miracle in his pocket that morning when he left home? Absolutely not. And it was not a miracle until he gave it to the Lord.

My friend, what is in your pocket? I am not talking about money. I'm talking about the pocket of your heart. What is in the pocket of your life that God would use to bless many others if you simply gave it to Him? Football coaches often tell their players, "Bring nothing back to the locker room; leave it all on the field." I think I can hear our Heavenly Head Coach crying to us from the Heavenly grandstand, "DO NOT COME TO HEAVEN WITH A MIRACLE IN YOUR POCKET; LEAVE IT ALL ON THE FIELD." Friend, please don't go to Heaven with a miracle in your pocket.

Unto Him Be Glory

~ 4 ~

The Saddest Words Jesus Ever Spoke

[21]Then said Jesus again unto them, I go my way, and ye shall seek me, and shall die in your sins: whither I go, ye cannot come. [22]Then said the Jews, Will he kill himself? because he saith, Whither I go, ye cannot come. [23]And he said unto them, Ye are from beneath; I am from above: ye are of this world; I am not of this world. [24]I said therefore unto you, that ye shall die in your sins: for if ye believe not that I am he, ye shall die in your sins.
(John 8:21-24)

Some years ago, I was preaching in revival services at a church in Huntsville, Alabama. One evening a man and his wife visited one of the services. They were noticeably different from other people in attendance. They were obviously from another country and were dressed in clothing that reflected their culture. They spoke English, but their accent made it difficult to understand everything they said. The next day the pastor and I went to visit the couple in their home. It was a large, beautiful home in a very exclusive part of that city. The man was not at home because he was at work. He was at that time a high-level employee at NASA, a part of the space industry.

The lady of the house invited us to come in, and we went into the family room of the home. The lady was very polite and gracious, but she was not a Christian. The pastor and I shared our testimonies with her and presented the plan of salvation. She smiled as we talked with her, but she did not receive the Lord into her heart.

She stood up and walked over to the fireplace and pointed to what I thought was a large silver tray on the mantle. Then she announced, "This is my god." She went on to inform us that in her native land she was a member of a shrine cult and that every member had their own god. I asked her if I might stand up and look at her god closely. She gave permission, so I walked over to that silver tray and looked at it for quite some time.

I asked the lady, "Where are your god's eyes?" She said, "He has none." I responded, "Then how does he see?" She did not reply. Then I asked, "Where are your god's ears?" She said, "He has no ears." I inquired, "Then how does he hear?" She said nothing. Finally, I asked, "Where is your god's mouth?" She answered, "He has no mouth." I responded, "Then how does he speak?" Again, there was no reply, not from her or her god. Neither one of them would talk to me. As I stood there looking at that piece of metal on the mantle, in my heart I thanked God for Jesus Who can see, hear, and speak.

Jesus speaks! The book of Hebrews opens with this declaration, *"God, who at sundry times and in divers manners spake in time past unto the fathers by the prophets, hath in these last days spoken unto us by his Son."* When you read the New Testament, some of the words of Jesus are heartwarming words. In the twenty-fourth chapter of Luke, we find his account of the resurrection. While Jesus did rise from the dead that Sunday morning, most people did not believe it. Even many of those who had been following Him could not accept the idea of His resurrection. They had seen Him beaten, crucified, and buried. Their hopes were dashed, and their dreams were destroyed.

With great discouragement many of those who had been by His side walked away from Jerusalem that morning. Two of those who walked away were men who lived in the town of Emmaus, which was about seven miles from Jerusalem. You can just see them slowly walking along, kicking the dust in defeat and talking sorrowfully. Suddenly, out of nowhere Jesus began walking with them. They are not able to recognize Him because their eyes are "holden" (verse 16). Their eyes were not allowed to recognize Him at that time.

Jesus asks them why they are so discouraged and talking so sadly? The men respond, "Did you just get off the bus? Don't you know what has been going on here?" Then they tell Him about the hope they had in a man named Jesus. They hoped He was going to be the redeemer of Israel, but the rulers had condemned Him and crucified Him. Then the Master Teacher gave them a Bible study as they continued walking. The men still did not recognize Him, but they listened intently. Jesus begins with the writings of Moses, goes through the writings of the prophets, and reveals to them what the Old Testament taught about the Messiah. The Messiah was going to suffer and die before entering into His glory.

When they arrive at Emmaus, the men take Jesus to their home for the evening meal. While they were eating, the men were given the ability to recognize the identity of their Visitor. As soon as they knew it was Jesus Who had been with them that day, He vanished out of their sight. He did not get up and leave the room, He vanished, disappeared. After His departure, the men said to one another, *"Did not our heart burn within us, while he talked with us by the way, and while he opened to us the scriptures?"* (verse 32). Heartwarming words!

Some of the words of Jesus were life-giving words. In the sixth chapter of John, there was another time when many were walking away from the Lord. He turned to the twelve and asked them if they, too, were going to go away. Their leader, Simon Peter, responded, *"Lord, to whom shall we go? thou hast the words of eternal life."* (verse 68).

In 1874, P.P. Bliss wrote, *"Christ, the blessed One, gives to all wonderful words of life; sinner, list to the loving call, wonderful words of life; all so freely given, wooing us to heaven: Beautiful words, wonderful words, wonderful words of life."* Life-giving words!

Then, some of the words of Jesus in the New Testament are encouraging words. Hear Him as He says, "Fear not." Listen carefully to Him as He boldly declares, "Be of good cheer." Give Him praise as He promises, "I will never leave you." Those words are uplifting words. They give us the courage to attack Hell with a water pistol. Encouraging words!

In the text for this sermon, Jesus is speaking to a group of Pharisees. The Pharisees of that day were like a lot of church members today; they have a lot of religion, but no real relationship with God. Religion has never been a friend to Christianity. Christianity is not a religion. Buddhism is a religion. Hinduism is a religion. Islam is a religion. Christianity is not a religion; it is a relationship with God through Jesus Christ.

The word *Pharisee* means separate or separated. The Pharisees thought they were right with God because they lived separated lives. There were certain foods they would not eat and certain places they would not go. There were certain people they would not associate with and certain things they would not do. Because they had separated themselves from these things, they believed that God was pleased with them. Unfortunately, in all their separatism, they had really separated themselves from God.

Jesus is speaking to these very religious, but very lost men. As He speaks, His words are not heartwarming words. His words are not life-giving words. His words are not encouraging words. Instead, His words to these Pharisees are the saddest words Jesus ever spoke. They are the saddest words He ever spoke because they reveal three very sad conditions.

I. A SAD WAY TO LIVE

In verse twenty-four, Jesus said, "for if ye believe not." That means to live without faith. God does not force His way into the life of anyone. If you choose to live without faith you have that right. You do not have to believe in Jesus or anything else. Some people refuse to believe in anything they cannot see, or feel, or hear, or taste, or smell. If it cannot be observed by the five senses, those folks will not believe in it. That is a choice you have to make, but if you choose to live without faith, there are certain, sure consequences that follow that choice.

Without Faith You Cannot Be Saved

The Apostle Paul stated, *"For by grace are ye saved through faith"* (Ephesians 2:8). It is grace that saves, not faith. Salvation has nothing to do with works; it is all of grace. God's grace does not come into a person's life through baptism. Grace does not enter your life by partaking of the Lord's Supper. God's amazing grace only comes into your life when you put your faith in Jesus Christ as Savior and Lord. Salvation is a free gift of God, but it can only be received through faith.

Without Faith You Cannot Please God

Hebrews 11:6 declares, *"But without faith it is impossible to please him* (God).*"* The writer did not say that it is hard to please God without faith. He said it is IMPOSSIBLE. It does not matter how nice or polite a person may be. It makes no difference how generous or supportive a person may be. It does not matter how many songs you sing, lessons you teach, or sermons you preach. Without faith you will never do anything or say anything or be anything that pleases God.

Without Faith You Will Never Have a Prayer Answered

Jesus said, *"And all things, whatsoever ye shall ask in prayer, believing, ye shall receive"* (Matthew 21:22). Note the word *believing*. It means *if you have faith*. Prayer without faith is not prayer at all. Faith is the key to answered prayer. The eloquence of our words does not impress God. Sentences with words like "Thee" and "Thou" do not capture the attention of God.

A heart of belief always has the ear of the Almighty. Pray as often as you like, ask God for anything you need, but always pray in faith. That is the way to get God's answers to your prayers. To live a faithless life is your privilege, but you will never be saved, you will never please God, and you will never have a prayer answered. That is a sad way to live!

II. A SAD WAY TO DIE

These words of Jesus are the saddest He ever spoke because they speak of a sad way to die. Three times in these four verses Jesus informs these Pharisees that they are going to die in their sins. Death is a universal experience. It is a sentence that was passed on the entire human family. Everybody dies, but everybody does not die in their sins. What does it mean to die in your sins?

To Die Having Never Experienced the Forgiveness of God

To die in your sins means you die having never experienced the forgiveness of God. Of all the doctrines in the Bible, the one that is most precious to me is the doctrine of the forgiveness of God. I am very glad God is a forgiving God. The word *forgive* means *to send away*. When God forgives you of your sins, He sends your sins away. There are three pictures of that in the Bible.

First, Psalm 103:12 says, *"As far as the east is from the west, so far hath he removed our transgressions from us."* How far is the east from the west? It is an immeasurable distance. You can measure the distance from the north to the south. Get a compass and start heading north and eventually you will come to the North Pole. Once you pass it, you will be heading south. Just keep on going and eventually you will come to the South Pole. When you pass it, you will be heading north. But you cannot measure the distance from east to west. You can get on an airplane and head east and circle the globe fifty times. All you are doing is heading east. Or, you can get on an airplane and head west and circle the globe fifty times. All you are doing is heading west. God has sent our sins away an immeasurable distance.

Second, in Isaiah 38:17 the prophet declared, *"for thou hast cast all my sins behind thy back."* God casts, hurls, throws our sins behind His back. That means the middle of His back. Have you ever tried to see the middle of your back? Even an Indian rubber man cannot turn his head that far. God has sent our sins to a place where He no longer sees them.

Third, the prophet Micah proclaimed, *"and thou wilt cast all their sins into the depths of the sea"* (Micah 7:19). God has cast all our sins—not some of them, but all of them--into the depths of the sea, never to be fetched up again. Drowned in the depths of the sea, they are gone forever.

So, where did God send our sins? Did He send them away as far as the east is from the west, or did He place them in the middle of His back, or did He cast them into the depth of the sea? The answer is YES. Just pick one; it does not matter. They are simply a picture that our sins are gone. Does that mean when God forgives, He forgets? No! God is omniscient and cannot forget. However, He chooses not to remember our sins anymore after He has sent them away. Hallelujah!

To Die with No Future Opportunity to be Saved

To die in your sins means that you die with no future opportunity to be saved. Some people erroneously believe that after death, somewhere in the dim, dark, dismal great beyond, God will appear before them and give them another opportunity to be saved. Friend, that is just not true. The Bible never even hints at such a thing. According to the sixteenth chapter of Luke, at death, saved people go to be with the Lord and lost people go to hell, and there is no moving from one place to the other. Do not make a mistake at this point. Eternity is too long to be wrong.

To Die with No Hope for Heaven

If a person dies in his or her sins, they have no hope of going to Heaven. The alarm needs to be sounded again: GOOD people do not go to Heaven, SAVED people go to Heaven. Heaven is a real place, and I'm looking forward not just to going there, but living there forever.

Just think about what is there: golden streets, gates of pearl and walls of jasper. No place like that down here. But also, think about what is not in Heaven:

no sickness, no pain, no death, and no sorrow. Wow! But those who die in their sins have no hope of going there. If you die in your sins and you have never experienced the forgiveness of God, you will have no more opportunity to be saved, and you have absolutely no hope for Heaven. That is a sad way to die!

III. A SAD WAY TO SPEND ETERNITY

The message of Jesus to these Pharisees was the saddest message He ever proclaimed because it spoke of a sad way to spend eternity. These verses reveal just how twisted and perverted religion can be. When Jesus told the Pharisees that He was going away and they could not go where He was going, their religion led them to a drastically wrong conclusion. They assumed that Jesus was going to commit suicide and go to Hell. The Pharisees believed and taught that all Jews go to Heaven when they die simply because they are Jews. According to them, the only way a Jew would not go to Heaven was to commit suicide. If a Jew took his own life, then he forfeited his right to go to Heaven. The Bible never teaches anything like that.

In their twisted thinking they knew they were going to Heaven because they were Jews. If Jesus, being a Jew, was going where they were not going, then He must be planning to kill Himself and go to Hell. How wrong they were! Where Jesus was going and where they were not going was to Heaven. They were going to Hell with all their religion and all their separatism.

55

There is not much preaching about Hell today, but God has not changed His mind. Hell is still very much in existence, and to end up there is a sad way to spend eternity.

Hell is a Place of Pain

The Bible teaches that there is literal, burning fire in Hell, but the fires in Hell are not like any other fires you have ever seen. All of us have seen fires. Campfires, grass fires, house fires, massive community fires, we've seen them all. But every fire you have ever seen in your life eventually stopped burning. Maybe it burned itself out, or you put it out with a hose, or the fire department came and extinguished it. But the fires of Hell never stop burning. In the ninth chapter of Mark, Jesus said five times that the fires of Hell are never quenched, they never cease to burn. O, the pain that those fires cause!

Hell is a Place of Sorrow

Today many people joke about Hell, but Hell is no joke. No one ever laughs or smiles there. No grins, no chuckles, no smirks in that horrible place. There are no light moments, no funny stories, or happy times in Hell. Jesus said that the sounds of Hell are weeping and wailing. Eternal sobbing and screaming are the sounds of Hell. No songs, no chirping of birds, no pitter-patter of children's feet. Only weeping and wailing. What griefs, what bitter regrets, and what heartaches fill that place of outer darkness.

Hell is a Place of Hatred

Seven times in the New Testament Jesus said that in Hell there is gnashing of teeth. Is there anything or anyone in your life that you hate so much that the very thought of it or them makes you begin to grind your teeth? That's gnashing of teeth. There is no love in Hell. No embraces, no kisses, no moonlight strolls are ever known there. Everybody hates God there, and everybody hates each other there.

Years ago, a man told me he wanted to go to Hell when he died. I inquired as to why. He told me that he wanted to go to Hell to see his Dad again. He said, "Preacher, I know my dad is in Hell. I saw him throw preachers out of our house when I was a boy. I saw him tear pages out of the Bible and blow his nose on them. I saw him drive to the church yard and use the bathroom on the parking lot. He despised all Christians and called them hypocrites. When he died, he died cursing God. I know he is in hell. But he was my best buddy when I grew up. My dad taught me how to hunt, fish, and play golf. He taught me how to drive a car. We went to all kinds of ball games together. I want to go to Hell to see my dad again." I told that man the best thing he could do for his dad would be to get saved. I told him if he went to Hell, he would curse his dad for all eternity and blame him for leading him to such a horrible place, and that his dad would hate him back. What an unbelievably awful place! What a sad way to spend eternity!

What sad words that came from the lips of Jesus! A sad way to live, a sad way to die, and a sad way to spend eternity. But it does not have to be that way. No one has to live without faith. No one has to die in their sins. No one has to spend eternity in Hell. If you will believe in Jesus as your Savior and Lord, you will not die in your sins, but in the sweet forgiveness of God, and you will not go to Hell but to Heaven. If you are not a child of God, repent of your sin and receive Jesus as the Lord of your life. Even the saddest words Jesus ever spoke remind us of a better way!

~ 5 ~

He Came Down

[17]And he came down with them, and stood in the plain, and the company of his disciples, and a great multitude of people out of all Judaea and Jerusalem, and from the sea coast of Tyre and Sidon, [18]which came to hear him, and to be healed of their diseases; And they that were vexed with unclean spirits: and they were healed. [19]And the whole multitude sought to touch him; for there went virtue out of him, and healed them all. (Luke 6:17-19)

Have you ever messed up? I don't mean messed up when cooking a cake or messed up when taking a test at school. Have you ever messed up in your Christian life? Have you ever said something you wish you had not said? Have you ever done something you wish you had not done? Have you ever harbored a grudge against someone you wish you didn't harbor? As a result, did you ever wish you could start over in your Christian life?

Louisa Fletcher expressed that idea in a poem:

I wish that there were some wonderful place
Called the Land of Beginning Again,
Where all our mistakes and all our heartaches
And all of our poor selfish grief
Could be dropped like a shabby old coat at the door
And never be put on again.

There is a place where you can start over in your Christian life. That place is in the presence of the Lord. In His presence you really can discover the Land of Beginning Again. You can be in His presence anywhere you establish an altar. It can be at church, at home, in your car, or outside under a tree.

I heard about a lady who told her pastor, "Preacher, I would love to have a family altar in my home, but I don't have room for any more furniture." The altar is not a piece of furniture. It is a place in your heart reserved for the Lord. You don't build an altar with wood and nails. You establish it in your heart by setting aside time to spend with God. He is never too busy for you, but are you too busy for Him? If you want to make a fresh start in your life, you must make time and take time to be alone with God in the altar of your heart.

The three verses in our text for this message are the three most overlooked, most neglected verses in the New Testament. There is something of a practical reason for that. These three verses are surrounded by significant passages of Scripture. In the first sixteen verses of the chapter, Jesus chooses the men who would be His original twelve disciples. That was a big deal. The Christianity we practice today is due in large part to the ministry of those early disciples.

Then, beginning in verse twenty and going through the rest of the chapter, we find one of the few recorded sermons of Jesus, "The Sermon on the Plain." That, too, was a big deal. Jesus was the greatest preacher that ever lived. No man ever spoke like He did. Yet, very few of His sermons are written down, but here is one of them.

So these three verses in our text get lost in the shuffle. Some even consider them to be insignificant. They have been called "nothing but connective tissue," joining together the selection of the twelve and "The Sermon on the Plain." Others say the only purpose of these three verses is to reveal how that crowd on the mountain got down to the plain. I hope you have a higher view of the inspiration of Scripture than that. Paul said, "*All scripture is given by inspiration of God, and is profitable for doctrine, for reproof, for correction, for instruction in righteousness"* (2 Timothy 3:16). If you will take a close look at these three verses you will find one of the best portraits of Jesus to be found in the Word of God.

I. HE CAME DOWN

Verse seventeen says, *"And he came down with them."* He had been up on a mountain, but He was not there alone. There was a great multitude on the mountain with Him. In the Christian life God allows us to have some mountaintop experiences, but the Christian life is not lived on the mountaintop. The Christian life is lived in the valley. In the ninth chapter of Luke, we find Jesus on another mountaintop with three of His disciples, James, Peter, and John. On that mountaintop Jesus did something that He never did again during His earthly ministry. He allowed His glory to shine through the very pores of His skin.

When Peter beheld the fulness of the glory of Jesus Christ, he asked Jesus to let the disciples stay on that mountain forever and never return to the valley. Jesus did not rebuke him, but made it clear that He and the disciples would return to the valley. It is in the valley that we serve the Lord. In the valley there are people who need our ministry. The valley is filled with ruined lives, wounded hearts, broken homes, and all kinds of sicknesses and afflictions. That is where we can be the salt of the earth and the light of the world. From time to time God lets us get on the mountain. There we can lift our hands and shout to the top of our voices in praise to Him. But He always leads us back to the valley to serve Him by serving others.

In Exodus 3:7-8, God said to Moses, *"I have surely seen the affliction of my people which are in Egypt, and have heard their cry by reason of their taskmasters; for I know their sorrows; And I am come down to deliver them."* He came down! In the third chapter of John, Jesus said to Nicodemus, *"And no man hath ascended up to heaven, but he that came down from heaven, even the Son of man which is in heaven"* (verse 13). He came down! In the sixth chapter of John, Jesus told us that He is the true bread of life that came down from Heaven. He came down! I am glad He came down, because if He had not come down, I could never go up. You see, He came down and took all our sins upon Himself and carried them to the cross. He came down to pay a debt He did not owe, because we had a debt we could not pay. Thank God He came down!

II. HE CAME DOWN TO BE HEARD

Verse seventeen tells us that the people who came from Judea and Jerusalem and Tyre and Sidon all came to HEAR Jesus. Jesus has something to say.

For nine years I had the privilege of being the Dean of the Adrian Rogers Center for Biblical Preaching at Mid-America Baptist Theological Seminary in Memphis, Tennessee. At times, students would ask how many points a sermon should have. My reply was, "At least one." I have heard a lot of sermons that had no point to them at all. Vance Havner used to

63

say, "I hate to go somewhere expecting beef steak and end up getting served Cool Whip.©"" Those who heard Jesus were never disappointed. He had something to say.

No matter what stage of life you may be in, Jesus has something to say to you. Jesus has something to say to children. He wants to tell boys and girls that He loves them and that He died to save them as well as anyone else. He wants to tell children that they do not need the permission of anyone to be saved. When He speaks to their hearts about sin and salvation, He is ready to save them. Of course, children need the approval of their parents concerning baptism and church membership, but they need no one's permission to be saved. He came down to be heard. Hear Him!

Jesus also has something to say to teenagers. He wants to talk to them about their sexuality. Yes, He has something to say about that. He wants to talk to teens about their choice of a life's mate. That is such an important decision. Do not leave Him out. He has something to say to young people about their life's vocation. He really does have a plan and purpose for each person. Also, Jesus wants to talk to teenagers about their attitude toward their parents. He came down to be heard. Hear Him!

Young adults, Jesus has something to say to you. He wants to talk to you about how to build a strong and happy marriage. He desires to speak to you concerning becoming godly parents. America has no greater need than godly dads and godly moms. Jesus also wants to talk to you about finances. More young marriages that end in divorce do so more often because of money than because of adultery. And young adults, the Lord has something to say to you about being faithful in your spiritual life. He came down to be heard. Hear Him!

Middle-aged adults need to hear from Him as well. He wants to talk to you about keeping your marriages strong and affair-proof. Jesus wants to talk to your age group about not allowing making money to become a god in your life. He has something to say to you about budgeting your time well so that you will not end up losing the most precious things in life. Also, Jesus wants to talk to middle-aged adults concerning how to live with teenagers. He came down to be heard. Hear Him!

Now we come to senior adults. I love senior adults. I am one! Jesus has something to say to our age group as well. He wants to talk to senior adults about making the rest of your life the best of your life. He wants to share some things with you about how to finish well. He also wants to let you know that it is perfectly okay to be excited about going to Heaven. Jesus also wants to tell you that you do not have to be afraid of CHANGE. To a lot of senior adults, change is a dirty word. Many of this age group do not like change and even resist it strongly. We want the same parking space and the same seat at church every Sunday. We do not like change.

Dear senior adult, do you know that the first thing God is going to do to you when you get to Heaven is change you? That is right, He is going to change you.

You may ask, "Why?" The answer is simple. The body that you now have is not suited for heavenly living. Your body is well suited for earthly living. You can live anywhere on this planet. Some places will be so cold you will need extra clothing, and some will be so hot you may have to remove some clothing, but you can live anywhere on earth. But your body is not suited for living in Heaven.

Paul dealt with that in 1 Corinthians 15. He says, *"All flesh is not the same flesh"* (verse 39). There is bird flesh and there is fish flesh. There is earthly flesh and there is heavenly flesh. In verse fifty-one, Paul states, *"Behold, I shew you a mystery; We shall not all sleep, but we shall all be CHANGED"* (emphasis mine). He gives two reasons why we must be changed.

First, our current bodies are CORRUPTIBLE. Corruptible means subject to decay. Our present bodies are subject to decay. Not only will our bodies decay in the grave, they are decaying right now. Did you know that most of the dust in your house is you? When you wipe off the dining room table, you are wiping off yourself. If you leave it alone for a few months, you can visit yourself. There will be no decay in Heaven. When God changes you, corruption will be replaced by incorruption.

Second, our bodies in which we now live are MORTAL. That means "subject to dying." Dying is not something we will do at the end of life; we are dying right now. Some people wear glasses. What happened to that part of their bodies that once gave them 20/20 vision? It died. Some people have gray hair. What happened to that part of their bodies that once gave them red or black or blond or brown hair? It died. Some people walk stooped over? What happened to that part of their bodies that once allowed them to walk upright? It died. Thank God, there will be no dying in Heaven. That is why this mortal will one day be replaced by immortality. He came down to be heard. Hear Him!

III. HE CAME DOWN TO
BE TOUCHED

Verse nineteen says, *"And the whole multitude sought to touch him."* They sought to touch Him, and He allowed them to touch Him. Today we live in an untouchable society. People just do not want to be touched. We go to extremes to avoid a personal touch. But Jesus was not an untouchable Savior. The only exception was on the morning of His resurrection, but by that evening, He once again allowed people to touch Him.

The Gospels of Mark and Luke tell us of a woman who had an issue of blood. She had been dealing with that condition for twelve years. That is a long time to be sick. At the beginning, she got out of bed one morning and noticed a few spots of blood on her bed linens. She thought nothing about it. She probably assumed that her fingernail had scratched her side during the night. The next morning there was a little more blood and the next, a little more. It became obvious she was hemorrhaging. She spent all her wealth on physicians, but never got better. That does not mean the physicians were quacks, it simply means they could not help her. After twelve years her body is now emaciated. Her body can no longer replace the amount of blood being lost. She is grossly anemic, and she is dying. You can live without eyes, ears, arms, and legs, but you cannot live without blood, *"For the life of the flesh is in the blood"* (Leviticus 17:11).

Someone told this poor lady about Jesus, the Healer, and that He was passing through her city on a certain day. If she could get to Jesus, maybe He could help her. I see her as she pushes herself up in her bed into a sitting position. Then she slowly pushes herself into a standing position. She is exhausted and now must rest. Next, she slowly walks to the door of her house. Again, she needs to rest, but she still has to get to town. Very carefully, very meticulously she places one foot in front of the other making her way to the city.

When she arrives, there is a large crowd lining the street on which Jesus will walk. No one steps aside and allows her to come to the front, so she elbows her way through the throng, finally reaching the front. However, when she gets to the front of the line, Jesus has already passed by. Because of the massive crowd, He is moving very slowly. She decides to just fall toward Him with her hand extended. If she can just touch Him maybe that will be enough. If not, she will lie down in the street and die. In a last-ditch effort, she falls in His direction and her fingers touch the hem of His garment. She touched the hem of HIM. At that moment, power came from the body of Jesus and flowed through her fingers, up her arm, and throughout her entire body. She was immediately healed of her illness.

Jesus inquired of His disciples, "Who touched me?" They must have been somewhat puzzled because everybody had been touching Him. The whole day had been like a parade with people pushing and shoving and grabbing at Him. But this was a different kind of touch. It was not a touch of curiosity; it was a touch of faith. Jesus knew that power had left His body. When He confronted the woman, He said the most wonderful word He ever said to a woman. He said, "Daughter." This woman had not only been healed physically, she had been saved spiritually. She was no longer just a certain woman. Now she was the daughter of God. She touched Him!

There is a wonderful Gospel song which says, "He touched me, O He touched me, and O, the joy that floods my soul." And there is another song that says, "He is here Hallelujah, He is here Amen. He is here you can touch Him, and you will never be the same." When you got saved, Jesus wrapped you up in His arms and touched you. In this Christian life there are times when you need to touch Him. You can touch Him when you are sick. You can touch Him when your heart is broken over unsaved loved ones or when children go astray. You can touch Him when you have financial problems. You can touch Him when you need to start over in your Christian life. Find that altar in your heart and get alone with Him. By faith, reach out and touch Him. When you do, you will have found that wonderful place called the Land of Beginning Again.

Unto Him Be Glory

~ 6 ~

Hallelujah, What a Savior

²⁹And Jesus departed from thence, and came nigh unto the sea of Galilee; and went up into a mountain, and sat down there. ³⁰And great multitudes came unto him, having with them those that were lame, blind, dumb, maimed, and many others, and cast them down at Jesus' feet; and he healed them: ³¹Insomuch that the multitude wondered, when they saw the dumb to speak, the maimed to be whole, the lame to walk, and the blind to see; and they glorified the God of Israel. (Matthew 15:29-31)

Jesus and His disciples had been in Phoenicia. It was the only time in His earthly ministry that He had been outside what is referred to as the Holy Land. Now they return back to the Sea of Galilee.

Most of His ministry at the sea had been around the northern shore, but according to the Gospel of Mark, this time they go to the southeastern area around the sea to Decapolis. This was a totally Gentile area. The people there were predominantly pagan. They had been greatly influenced by the worship of Greek gods that only existed in the minds of ungodly people. But they had heard about Jesus, especially His ability to heal.

In Mark chapter five, Jesus encountered a man in Gadara that was demon possessed. The demons inside this man had turned him into a dangerous maniac. He lived in the graveyard, ran naked through the streets, was constantly cutting himself, and viciously attacked anyone who tried to restrain him. He had super-human strength provided him by the demons within. He could easily break chains that bound him.

Jesus cast the demons out of the man, and as a result, this tragic man was set free. He was, *"sitting, and clothed, and in his right mind"* (Mark 5:15). Verse twenty tells us that this man, after the demons were cast out by the Lord, departed from that place, and went to Decapolis, and told everyone there what Jesus had done for him. This explains how those pagan Gentiles had heard of the ability of Jesus to heal.

When the people of Decapolis hear that Jesus has come into their territory, they seek Him and find Him on a mountainside. They come to Him in great multitudes, by the thousands, and they bring with them their loved ones and friends who needed to be healed.

I. THE CONDITION OF THOSE NEEDING HEALING

The first mentioned in that group that were carried or dragged up the mountain to where Jesus was are identified as the lame. These are people whose legs are attached to their bodies, but whose legs are crippled. They have legs, but they cannot walk as normal people. Perhaps they were born with a deformity, or they may have been crippled by an accident or an illness.

The blind were mentioned second. Some of these people had never seen at all, having been blind from birth. Others had lost their sight as a result of an act of violence or an unfortunate mishap. Either way, these folks groped in darkness all the time.

Next are the dumb. These are people who were without the ability to speak. They could not talk, sing, shout, or even whisper. They lived in silence.

The maimed were the fourth group. Some versions translate this word as "crippled." But these people were more than just crippled. The maimed were those who had no legs or arms. They may have been like this as a result of a birth defect or maybe a serious injury in battle.

Finally, Matthew adds *"and many others"* (verse 30). This would include any other handicap, sickness, or affliction not covered in the first four. All in all, this was a pathetic group of people.

II. THE LOCATION OF THESE PEOPLE

Matthew tells us that the people who brought these who needed healing, *"cast them down at Jesus' feet"* (verse 30). That does not mean they laid them at Jesus' feet or placed them at Jesus' feet. They cast them, hurled them, threw them at His feet. There was such a sense of urgency and there were so many coming up the mountain with others that needed the power of Jesus in their lives, no time was wasted, and no etiquette was followed. They were cast at the feet of Jesus. The Bible says a lot about the feet of Jesus. As a matter of fact, more is said about His feet than any other part of His anatomy.

Bruised Feet

His feet are bruised feet. In the third chapter of Genesis, the darkest chapter in the Bible, we find the entrance of Satan and sin on planet earth. God had placed Adam and Eve in a perfect environment, the Garden of Eden. There was nothing lacking in that beautiful garden. Everything worked in perfect harmony with everything else. There were no thorns or thistles. There was nothing to fear. God had filled the garden with fruit bearing trees. He gave Adam and Eve permission to eat all they wanted from any tree in the garden except one. There really was not anything different about that tree. The fruit was no better, no bigger, and no sweeter than on any other tree. That tree was simply a sign of God's sovereignty over the original couple. God told them disobedience would bring sudden death.

Satan came into the garden in the disguise of a serpent. He approached Eve and asked her what God had said. She told him that God had said that she and Adam could eat of any tree in the garden except one. If they disobeyed God and ate from the forbidden tree, they would die that very same day. Satan told Eve that God was holding out on her and her mate. The reason they were told not to eat from that tree was because God knew if they ate the fruit of that tree, they would become gods themselves. Satan also told her that they would not die if they ate from that tree.

Eve ate the forbidden fruit, and when Adam arrived, he also ate it. They had sinned against God by disobeying Him, but they did not die. It looked as though God had lied and Satan had told the truth, but that can never happen. It is impossible for God to lie, and it is impossible for Satan to tell the truth. Adam and Eve did not die physically, but they died spiritually the moment they rebelled against God.

When God came into the garden that day, He already knew what had happened. Adam attempted to blame Eve for what had happened, and Eve tried to blame the serpent. God then gave the first prophecy of Jesus Christ in the Bible as He addresses the devil in Genesis 3:15, *"And I will put enmity between thee and the woman, and between thy seed and her seed; it shall bruise thy head, and thou shalt bruise his heel."* God speaks of the seed of a woman. Women do not have seed, men have seed. Women have eggs. The seed of a woman refers to a virgin birth. God declares to the devil that one day there will be One, born of a virgin, Who will bruise and crush his head. That virgin-born man is Jesus Christ. When Jesus was on the cross, the devil bruised His heel, but when Jesus rose from the dead, He bruised the head of Satan. It is often said that the devil is alive and well on planet earth, but not so. He may be alive, but he is not well. He has a seriously bruised head that will one day bring about his downfall. The bruised feet of Jesus speak of our salvation through His atoning death.

Beautiful Feet

The feet of Jesus are beautiful feet. In Isaiah 52:7, the prophet spoke of the coming Messiah over seven hundred years before He came when he said, *"How beautiful upon the mountains are the feet of him that bringeth good tidings, that publisheth peace; that bringeth good tidings of good, that publisheth salvation."* The Apostle Paul brought that into the New Testament in Romans 10:15, *"How beautiful are the feet of them that preach the gospel of peace, and bring glad tidings of good things."* The greatest preacher of all time was not Billy Sunday or Billy Graham, but Jesus Christ. His feet are beautiful feet.

Beloved Feet

76

His feet are beloved feet. In the seventh chapter of Luke, Jesus goes to the house of Simon the Pharisee for supper. Simon did not invite Jesus to his home because he liked Him or wanted to know Him better. He wanted to discredit Jesus and that is why he brought Jesus into his home. When Jesus arrived, He saw that many other Pharisees were there. They all watch Him with critical eyes and listen to Him with critical ears.

As they sat on the floor eating supper an uninvited and unwanted woman enters the house. Without question this woman had been a prostitute. All her life she had been used and abused by wicked men. Sometime before this supper event, Jesus had met this woman, had forgiven her of all her sin, and had saved her by His grace. When she saw Jesus go into Simon's house, she follows Him. You can hear the gasps of the Pharisees as she enters the room. She goes to the feet of Jesus and washes His feet with her tears, then dries them with her hair. Then she starts kissing the feet of Jesus again and again. She was loving His feet.

In John eleven, Jesus raised Lazarus from the dead. In chapter twelve, Jesus goes into the home of Lazarus and his two sisters, Mary and Martha. While supper is being served, Mary breaks an expensive container of very fragrant ointment and anoints the feet of Jesus. When Judas sees this, he rebukes Mary for wasting something that could have been sold and the proceeds given to the poor. Of course, Judas could care less about the poor; he was only seeing dollar signs. Jesus then rebukes Judas. Mary was simply loving the feet of Jesus. His feet were beloved feet.

77

Blessing Feet

The Lord's feet are blessing feet. In Mark five Jairus, a ruler of the synagogue, falls at the feet of Jesus and tells Him about his twelve-year-old daughter who is dying. Jairus pleads with Jesus to go home with him and heal his daughter. Jesus agrees to go.

As they are making their way to that house, they encounter a group that tells them the girl is dead. Jesus and Jairus go on to the house where Jesus raised the little girl from the dead. That was victorious, but the blessing came when Jairus was at the feet of Jesus earlier. Blessing feet!

In the seventh chapter of Mark, Jesus was in Phoenicia. A Canaanite woman approaches Him and falls at His feet. She tells Him that she is the mother of a demon-possessed girl. After some interesting dialogue for the benefit of the disciples, Jesus tells the woman that the demon is now gone from her daughter. When she got home, she found that what Jesus said to her while she was at His feet was true. Blessing feet!

Brass Feet

The feet of Jesus are also brass feet. In the first chapter of the Revelation, we find the Apostle John exiled on the island of Patmos. He is now an old man, about a hundred years old. He has been put on that island as a punishment because he would not stop preaching the Gospel.

On a Sunday morning Jesus appears before John, but He is unlike John remembered Him. His hair was white like wool, His eyes were as pools of fire, a sharp double-edged sword proceeded out of His mouth, *"And his feet like unto fine brass, as if they burned in a furnace"* (verse 15). These are the judgment feet of the Lord, trampling out the vintage where the grapes of wrath are stored. Those who refuse to come to his feet for the blessing of salvation will one day be trampled beneath His feet of judgement.

III. THE DEMONSTRATION OF JESUS

As the people were cast at the feet of Jesus, the Bible says, *"and he healed them"* (Matthew 15:30). What sublime simplicity! There were no trumpets blasting, no angels singing, no fanfare at all; he just healed them. The lame were walking, the blind were seeing, the dumb were speaking, and the maimed were made whole. Made whole! Those who had no legs miraculously grew them, instantaneously. Those who had no arms were now clapping their hands. Made whole! Hallelujah, what a Savior! No power can overcome Him. No demon can defeat Him. No army can conquer Him. No government can eliminate Him. He is Lord! He is in charge! He is the boss!

IV. THE CELEBRATION THAT FOLLOWED

Matthew says, *"and they all glorified the God of Israel"* (verse 31). People began praising God, the God of Israel. Remember who these people were. They were pagans who worshipped false gods. They had no affinity for nor loyalty to the God of Israel, but look at them now, praising the God of Israel. What happened? Jesus showed up! Everything changes when Jesus shows up. The fat lady cannot sing until He shows up. The final curtain cannot drop until He shows up. He is never a sideshow. Jesus is always the main attraction.

Many of the pagans had gotten born again that day. They were not just praising with their lips; they were praising with their hearts. The greatest miracles that took place that day were not external, but internal. The gods of wood and stone had never done anything for these people, but Jesus changed their lives and changed their destinies.

I wish I had been there to see that. I like to think that some television broadcaster might have been there, someone like Wolf Blitzer of CNN News.

I see him as he approaches a man and says, "Sir, I see you are praising the God of Israel today. You have never done that before. What's going on?"

I hear the man respond, "Wolf, do you see that little girl over there singing to the top of her voice? That is my daughter. She has never spoken a word in her life. Today I brought her up this mountain and cast her at the feet of Jesus, and He healed her. Wolf, Jesus is the God of Israel. Just look at my little girl. That's why I'm praising Him."

Then Wolf sees a lady and interviews her. "Ma'am, I see you are praising the God of Israel. Can you tell me why?"

She says, "Yes sir, I can tell you why. Do you see that woman over there surrounded by all those children? That is my mother. When my brothers and sisters and I were children, our mother lost her eyesight, and she had never seen any of her grandchildren. Today I brought her to Jesus and He gave her sight. All those children over there with her are her grandchildren. Look at her! She is seeing them for the very first time, and she is so happy. Jesus did that for her. He is the God of Israel. Look at my mother; that's why I'm praising the God of Israel."

A third person steps up to talk with Wolf, a gentleman. Wolf investigates, "Sir, can you tell me why you are praising the God of Israel?"

He replies, "O yes. Do you see that little boy over there jumping up and down and running around? That is my son. He has been crippled all his life. He has never taken a single step or even stood alone. All his life we have had to carry him everywhere he went, but today I brought him to Jesus, and He healed my son. Jesus is the God of Israel. Look at my boy; that's why I'm praising the God of Israel."

81

The amazed television reporter comes to one more woman and asks her why she is praising the God of Israel. She says, "Mr. Blitzer, do you see that older gentleman over there doing jumping jacks and kicking his legs higher than his head? That is my dad. Years ago, my dad went off to war and was severely wounded in his legs. Gangrene set in and the military doctor told him that it was either his legs or his life. My dad's legs were amputated just below his hips, and for all these years he has been an invalid. All he has been able to do is scoot around on his nubs. Today I dragged him to Jesus, and something unusual happened. If I had not seen it with my own eyes, I would not have believed it. Jesus touched him, and suddenly he grew two full grown legs—brand new legs. Jesus is the God of Israel. Look at my dad; that's why I'm praising the God of Israel."

Man of sorrows what a name
For the Son of God who came,
Ruined sinners to reclaim,
Hallelujah, what a Savior.

Bearing shame and scoffing rude,
In my place condemned He stood,
Sealed my pardon with His blood,
Hallelujah, what a Savior.

Guilty, vile and helpless we,
Spotless Lamb of God was He,
Full atonement can it be,
Hallelujah, what a Savior.

Lifted up was He to die,
It is finished was His cry,
Now in Heaven exalted high,
Hallelujah, what a Savior.

When He comes our glorious King,
All His ransomed home to bring,
Then anew this song we'll sing,
Hallelujah, what a Savior.
                                   -P.P. Bliss

~7 ~

The Widow's Two Mites

⁴¹And Jesus sat over against the treasury, and beheld how the people cast money into the treasury: and many that were rich cast in much. ⁴²And there came a certain poor widow, and she threw in two mites, which make a farthing. ⁴³And he called unto him his disciples, and saith unto them, "Verily I say unto you, that this poor widow hath cast more in than all they which have cast into the treasury: ⁴⁴For all they did cast in of their abundance; but she of her want did cast in all that she had, even all her living."
(Mark 12:41-44)

The events recorded in this text took place on a Tuesday morning, but not just any Tuesday morning. It was the last Tuesday morning of His life and His last appearance in the temple before His death. On Friday morning, only seventy-two hours away, He is going to be crucified.

He had entered Jerusalem on the previous Sunday riding a donkey. The people laid palm branches in the donkey's path as a way of honoring the One riding him. They shouted, *"Hosanna: Blessed is he that cometh in the name of the Lord: Blessed be the kingdom of our father David, that cometh in the name of the Lord: Hosanna in the highest"* (Mark 11:9-10). With such high praise it is no wonder this is often referred to as the triumphal entry of Jesus into Jerusalem. However, it should be remembered that these same people on Friday will be shouting, "Crucify him, crucify him." After a brief time in the Temple, Jesus returned to Bethany for the evening.

Early Monday morning Jesus went back to the city. On His way there, He cursed the barren fig tree. Arriving at the Temple, He became enraged by those who were prostituting the House of God, using it for their own personal gain. Jesus turned over the tables of the moneychangers and drove them out of the Temple. He accused them of turning the House of Prayer into a den of thieves. Then He returned to the town of Bethany.

On Tuesday morning Jesus and the disciples go back into the city once again. As they pass by the fig tree He had cursed the day before, the disciples point out to Jesus that it had withered away from the roots. Jesus instructs them to be men of faith who will trust God in all things, not men who just look at fig trees, and they continue to the Temple.

Jesus encounters four delegations on His way to the Temple who challenge Him at different points. The first delegation was made up of chief priests, scribes, and elders. This group was from the Sanhedrin, the Jewish Supreme Court. They were men of authority. They made the laws, and they saw to it that their laws were strictly enforced. They were the final authority, and there was no higher court that could handle any appeals. As expected, they approach Jesus and challenge His authority.

These men are both angry and afraid of Jesus. He is a real threat to them and their power. They inquire of Him, *"By what authority doest thou these things? And who gave thee this authority to do these things* (Mark 11:28)? These men were members of the Sanhedrin, the only authoritative body around, and they were the men who held that authority tightly in their grip. They demanded to know what and who gave Jesus His authority. Their mission ended in defeat and they depart from Him, wanting to see Him dead.

The second delegation consisted of Pharisees and Herodians. These were the two major political groups in the land. We have Democrats and Republicans. The people of that day had Pharisees and Herodians. Oh, this was a crafty bunch. They precede their challenge with a bucket full of false flattery, hoping to throw Jesus off His guard but He was much too sharp for these stump babblers. They challenge the politics of Jesus. They ask Him a question dealing with the hottest political potato of that day, *"Is it lawful to give tribute to Caesar, or not? Shall we give, or shall we not give"* (Mark 12:14,15)? Jesus dismisses this bunch with a quip about a coin, and off they go befuddled.

Then Jesus encounters the third delegation. These are the Sadducees, the resident theologians, and they come to challenge the theology of Jesus. How these guys got to be the theologians of the day was a mystery because they did not believe anything. Especially, they did not believe in a resurrection. This was at the very heart of Jesus' theology. Can you imagine Christianity without the resurrection? They frame their question in the context of a silly story.

According to their story, there was a family in which there were seven brothers. The first brother married a woman, but he died before his wife conceived and brought forth a child. Moses taught that in a situation like that, the dead man's brother was to marry his widow and have a child by her. So the second brother married her, but he died before she could conceive and bring forth a child. Next, the third brother married her, and he died before she conceived. Then the fourth brother, the fifth brother, and the six brothers all did the same as the first three. They all died before she conceived and gave birth to a child.

Now it is the seventh brother's turn to marry this woman. Don't forget, this is not a true story, but a silly story made up by these all-wise theologs. Yes, it has now come time for this seventh brother, who has already attended the funeral services of his six older brothers, to marry this woman.

Friend, if I had been that seventh brother, I would have been on a bus out of town. There is no way I would have married that gal. I would not have even carried her out for a Dr. Pepper. But according to their fable, he marries her and meets the same fate. He dies before conception in her womb. So she has seven husbands in the hereafter. Finally, the woman dies and now here comes the question that is supposed to forever discredit the Son of God. *"In the resurrection therefore, when they shall rise, whose wife shall she be of them? For the seven had her to wife"* (Mark 12:23).

These cap and gown idiots were so proud of themselves. They had put Him under their thumbs and were waiting to watch Him squirm as He sought an answer. This was something that one day they could cheerfully describe to their grandchildren. But Jesus was not intimidated by these pinheads. He blew them away by telling them that they were ignorant. They were ignorant of the Scripture, and they were ignorant of God's power. He informed them that there was no marrying or giving in marriage in Heaven, and that the power of God guarantees a coming resurrection.

Finally, the fourth delegation—a one-man delegation—confronts Jesus. He is a lawyer, a scribe, an expert in the law of Moses. He comes to challenge Jesus' knowledge of the law. Matthew's Gospel tells us that this fellow was himself a Pharisee, and that he had been put up to confronting Jesus by the other Pharisees. This lawyer asks Jesus which commandment, which law, was the most important. If Jesus could not answer that question, He could not possibly be the Messiah. But Jesus did answer the question. *"The first of all the commandments is, Hear, O Israel, the Lord our God is one Lord: And thou shalt love the Lord thy God with all thy heart, and with all thy soul, and with all thy mind, and with all thy strength: This is the first commandment. And the second is like, namely this, Thou shall love thy neighbor as thyself"* (Mark 12:29-31). Jesus not only answered the lawyer's question, He did him one better. The scribe had no choice but to admit that Jesus had answered the question correctly.

After all these challenges Jesus enters the Temple and goes into the Court of the Women. The Court of the Women was a large courtyard approximately two hundred feet square. It was not called the Court of the Women because only women were there. Both men and women gathered in this Court to worship and give their offerings. It was called the Court of the Women because that was as far as women were allowed to go in the Temple. Men could go further, but not women.

Jesus, being emotionally drained from all the previous challenges, is sitting down. Mark says He sat over against the treasury. The treasury consisted of thirteen large offering baskets placed around the walls of the Court of the Women. The baskets were shaped like trumpets, large on the bottom and smaller at the top. Nine of them were for designated offerings and the other four were for freewill offerings. To sit over against the treasury means that Jesus was sitting in a position from which He could see all thirteen baskets at the same time. Through His direct vision and His peripheral vision, He could see who was giving and how much they were giving. Through His omniscience He also knew why they were giving. He still does!

On this particular day, a number of wealthy people came to give their offerings at the same time. Josephus was a prominent historian at that time. He was not a Jew or a Christian. He was a Roman, but was respected as a historian. He recorded that when wealthy people came to give their offerings, they employed trumpet players to go before them blasting away. They wanted to gain the attention of all onlookers. They wanted everyone to be impressed by their generosity. They were not really giving out of devotion to God, but out of devotion to themselves. Mark says that many of the rich people gave much. That means they gave a lot of money. Many of them probably paraded by all thirteen baskets, putting in large amounts. After they gave, they no doubt huddled in a corner congratulating each other on what they had done. They sure were proud of themselves, and they were sure God was proud of them too.

Then the scene changes. No trumpets are blasting, and no one is pompously passing by the baskets dropping in massive amounts of money. The only sound heard was the shuffle of the feet of an old lady whom Mark identifies as a poor widow. She goes only to one basket and drops in two mites which make a farthing. It was the least amount the law allowed a person to give. If you want to know how much a farthing is, divide seventeen cents by ninety-six. It comes out to .00177. You could not buy a used piece of chewing gum with what she put in that basket. I'm sure the rich folks chuckled as they saw her gift. They know God must surely be glad that they showed up. Otherwise, God would have gone bankrupt.

When Jesus saw what the woman had done, He summoned His disciples to His side. He said, "Did you men see that? Did you see what she did?" Then He made an astounding announcement, *"this poor widow hath cast more in, than all they which have cast into the treasury"* (verse 43). This poor widow has given more than all the wealthy people gave put together. The disciples must have been puzzled. How could that be? How could He say that? Did He flunk first grade arithmetic? Has He no understanding of finances? Does He know nothing about the value of money?

Then Jesus explains why He made His statement, *"For all they* (the rich) *did cast in of their abundance; but she of her want did cast in all that she had, even all her living"* (verse 44). The wealthy had given large amounts, but it did not cost them anything. They gave out of their abundance. They would not miss a single meal. They would not lose a single luxury. They simply gave God a tip, but not this widow. She gave everything she had. There was no more at home in a sugar bowl. She could not go to the bank and draw out more. She gave everything, all her livelihood. She sure made an impression on Jesus! Even though it was His last day in the Temple, it was a good day. Note three takeaways from this wonderful experience.

I. GOD DOES NOT SEE THINGS THE WAY WE SEE THEM

God does not always see things the way we see them. Let me rephrase that. God hardly ever sees things the way we see them. God looks at things from a heavenly point of view. We look at things from an earthly point of view. If we had been in the Court of the Women that morning, we would have been overwhelmed by the generosity of the rich and underwhelmed at the paltry amount given by the widow. We would have admired the great faithfulness of the rich and been embarrassed by the lack of commitment of the widow. But God does not always see things the way we do.

In the third chapter of the Revelation, Jesus sent a letter to the church at Sardis. That church had a great reputation. "Thou hast a name," Jesus said to them. Everybody was talking about the Sardis church, and the talk was positive. The church at Sardis was considered a church that had a lot on the ball. They were always going and doing and were filled with all kinds of activities. The whole community declared, "That Sardis church is an ALIVE church." That was the view through earthly eyes. But when the Great Physician examined them, His diagnosis was short and to the point. He said, "Thou art DEAD." That was from a heavenly point of view. He does not always see the things the way we do.

In that same chapter Jesus sent a letter to the church at Laodicea. Their problem had nothing to do with the way other people saw them, but with the way they saw themselves. They were pleased by their middle of the road approach to everything. They were never too hot or too cold. They were always on an even keel in all matters. Besides, they never wanted to ruffle any feathers because they did not want to offend the big givers. When the members looked at their church, they said, "Look at us. We are the kind of church all churches would like to be. We have lots of money, lots of programs, and have need of nothing. We are a healthy church." That was from their earthly point of view. But when the Lord looked at them, He said, "You make me sick. You are wretched, poor, miserable, blind, and naked." He saw them from a heavenly point of view. He does not always see things the way we see them.

In the Gospel of Luke, we find two men who went to the same place, at the same time, for the same purpose. One of those men was a publican, a tax collector. The other was a Pharisee, a man of religion with lots of braggadocio. These two men go to the Temple at an hour of prayer. The Pharisee, with all his religious façade, struts down to the front and tells God what a good man he is. He informs God, "*I thank thee, that I am not as other men are, extortioners, unjust, adulterers, or even as this publican. I fast twice in the week, I give tithes of all that I possess"* (Luke 18:11-12). Wow, what a guy! Most churches would have his name on the dotted line quick. He would make a great member. On the other hand, the publican stayed in the back, looked at the floor, beat upon his chest, and prayed, *"God be merciful to me a sinner"* (verse 13). No church would be eager to sign him up.

Jesus said one of those men went home from church saved, and the other went home lost. Surely there is no confusion about which was which. The Pharisee with all his self-righteousness and all his good deeds, was surely the saved man. And the publican who was without any sense of religious decorum must be the lost man. That is the conclusion that comes when looking through earthly eyes. But Jesus does not look through the eyes of earth, He looks through the eyes of Heaven. It was the Pharisee who went home lost and the Publican who went home saved. God does not always see things the way we see them.

II. GIVING IS NOT ABOUT MONEY, IT'S ABOUT THE HEART

The second principle from this event is about giving. Contrary to popular opinion, giving is not a matter of money; it is a matter of the heart. Mark says these rich people gave "much," but Jesus said the widow gave "mucher." There is no such word as "mucher," but when I need a word, I make it up. Every word in the dictionary was made up by somebody, and I have as much right as they do to make one up. They gave God a tip. Please don't let your life be a tip to God. He deserves our all, not just a part.

This poor widow woman was not a tipper in spiritual matters. She was all in. She gave everything with no second thoughts. She knew a truth I wish every Christian knew. She knew that her livelihood did not depend on what she had in her pocketbook, but on the faithfulness of God. Do you trust Him that much? Does your Christianity have that kind of confidence in God? The refrain of the hymn, "Great is Thy Faithfulness" says it well:

Great is Thy faithfulness! Great is Thy faithfulness!
Morning by morning new mercies I see:
All I have needed Thy hand hath provided,
Great is Thy faithfulness, Lord unto me!
                                                   -Thomas Chisholm

III. LITTLE IS MUCH WHEN GOD IS IN IT

There are many victories in the Bible that were won with few resources. David fell Goliath with a rock and a slingshot. Shamgar slew 600 Philistines with an ox goad. Samson killed 1,000 Philistines with the jawbone of an ass. Gideon and his little band of 300 soldiers destroyed 135,000 Midianites. Little is much when God is in it. The issue is not do you have all of Him, but does He have all of you.

Friend, young people today talk about leaning into God. That means let God have all your life, nothing held back. Trust Him to use you to do everything He saved you to do. He will, if you give Him the opportunity.

~ 8 ~

Be Glad in the Lord

*¹¹Be glad in the LORD, and rejoice, ye righteous:
and shout for joy, all ye that are upright in heart.*
(Psalm 32:11)

If I were to ask you, "What is the greatest verse in the New Testament?" you would probably reply, "John 3:16." That would be an excellent answer. That might not be your favorite verse in the New Testament, and it might not be your personal life verse. Many Christians have selected a verse of Scripture as a life verse. My life verse is, *"For we preach not ourselves, but Christ Jesus the Lord; and ourselves your servants*

for Jesus' sake" (2 Corinthians 4:5). But without doubt, the greatest verse in the New Testament is John 3:16. It reveals the greatest love the world has ever known *(For God so loved the world)*, the greatest gift that has ever been given (*that he gave his only begotten Son*), the greatest invitation ever extended (*that whosoever believeth in Him*), and the greatest promise ever made (*should not perish, but have everlasting life*).

If I were to ask you, however, "What is the greatest verse in the Old Testament?" your response might not come as quickly as John 3:16. To decide the greatest verse in the Old Testament might require some pondering time.

I do not pretend to tell you what the greatest verse in the Old Testament is, but I will tell you that Psalm 32:11 should be somewhere close to the top. Psalm 32:11 is a Gospel seed, planted in the heart of the Old Testament, that does not come to full fruition until you get to the New Testament. There is more New Testament truth in this verse than in any other Old Testament verse I have ever discovered. It is a verse that is full of Jesus and should make our hearts want to shout, "UNTO HIM BE GLORY!"

There are two major reasons why this verse is so significant. First, it tells us who we are as Christians. In my travels, I have discovered that many Christians have no idea who they really are. They walked an aisle, shook a hand, filled out a card, were baptized and became members of a church. That is what they did, but that is not who we are.

Second, this verse is extremely important because it tells us what we are to be doing as Christians. Many Christians have no clue concerning what they are supposed to be doing as followers of Jesus. If we could ever get a grasp on WHO we are and WHAT we are supposed to be doing, revival would break out in our churches!

I. WHO WE ARE AS CHRISTIANS

Our Christian identity is vitally important to our faith. We are not playing hide-and-seek, and we are not lambs parading as wolves. Who we are is a big deal. In Psalm 32:11, we find a threefold description concerning who we are.

We are in the Lord

A Christian is a person who is in the Lord. The verse does not say, "in the denomination." You may call yourself a Baptist, a Methodist, a Catholic, or a Pentecostal, but being in a denomination does not mean you are in the Lord. Neither does this verse say, "in the church." There are a lot of local church members who have never been saved and are not in the Lord. Also, Psalm 32:11 does not say, "in the class." There are many people who are enrolled in Bible classes who are not in the Lord.

The expression "in the Lord" was the favorite expression of the Apostle Paul. As a matter of fact, he used that expression over 160 times in the New Testament. If God says something one time, that is

101

enough. If He says something two times, that is more than enough. But if God says something over 160 times, we better get the message. Sometimes Paul said, "in Christ," and at times he said, "in Jesus." There were instances when he said, "in Christ Jesus," and at other times, "in Jesus Christ." Sometimes he used simpler terms like "in the Lord" or "in Him." All these terms mean the same thing. A Christian is a person who is in the Lord.

The Christian life has its beginning in the Lord

In 2 Corinthians 5:17, the Apostle Paul declared, *"Therefore if any man be in Christ, he is a new creature: old things are passed away; behold, all things are become new."* Notice, the word "new" is used two times, but not until after he says, "if any man (person) be IN CHRIST." The Christian life does not begin in the baptistry or at the Lord's Supper table. The Christian life begins when a person comes to be "in Christ." That is where and when the "new" begins.

The Christian life finds its assurance in the Lord

One of the most sublime verses in the Bible is stated with eloquent simplicity. It says, *"There is therefore now no condemnation to them which are in Christ Jesus, who walk not after the flesh, but after the Spirit"* (Romans 8:1). Did you see that? NO CONDEMNATION! Those are two of the sweetest words in Scripture. Who are the ones that will not face the condemnation of God? Paul shouts it out, "them which are IN CHRIST JESUS." As a Christian, I do not go to bed at night wondering if I will face the condemnation of God during the night. I do not wake up in the morning wondering if I will face the condemnation of God during the day. If a person dies without being in Christ, the only thing he will face for all eternity is the condemnation of God. But those who are in Christ Jesus have been promised "no condemnation."

*The Christian life is guaranteed God's eternal
 affection in the Lord*

First Corinthians 13 may be the greatest statement in Scripture concerning human love, but Romans 8:38-39 just may be the greatest statement in the Bible concerning God's love. It says, *"For I am persuaded, that neither death, nor life, nor angels, nor principalities, nor powers, nor things present, nor things to come, nor height, nor depth, nor any other creature, shall be able to separate us from the love of God, which is in Christ Jesus our Lord."* Nothing can separate a person that is "in Christ Jesus" from the love of God. Nothing in life or death, nothing in the spirit world, nothing in time, nothing in space, or anything else imaginable can separate a Jesus follower from the love of God. Nothing! Absolutely nothing!

"Well, preacher, doesn't God love everybody?" He surely does, but He does not love everybody the same. He loves the world of unsaved people with a genuine, strong love, but it is a temporary love. When a person dies without Christ and ends up in Hell, God's love for that person comes to an end There is no semblance of the love of God in Hell. God's love for His children, however, is an eternal love. That eternal love is real, but it is not extended to us because we are warm, cuddly, fuzzy folks, but because we are "in Christ Jesus."

Being "in the Lord" is a big deal, right? It sure is a big deal. It is where you became a brand-new person, where you were assured you will never face the condemnation of God, and where you were promised you will never be out of His love.

"Then tell me, preacher, how does a person get 'in the Lord?'" To be honest, it is one of the great mysteries in the Word of God. There is no formula or ten-step program to accomplish it. Let me give a personal testimony at this point.

When I was a thirteen-year-old boy, the Holy Spirit convicted me of my sins and pointed me to Jesus Christ as the only Savior. I repented of my sin and asked Jesus Christ to come into my life to be my Savior and Lord. When He came into me, somehow, mysteriously, miraculously, I ended up in Him. Unto Him be Glory!

We are Righteous

Psalm 32:11, says, *"rejoice, YE RIGHTEOUS"* (emphasis mine). A Christian is a person that God identifies as righteous. That is who you are as a child of God—you are righteous. That does not refer to self-righteousness. The prophet Isaiah gave God's view of self-righteousness in Isaiah 64:6, *"But we are all as an unclean thing, and all our righteousnesses are as filthy rags."* The word "righteousnesses" refers to all of our self-righteousness. All of our "righteousnesses" put together, all of them are as filthy rags.

The expression "filthy rags" refers to a menstrual cloth worn by a woman during her monthly cycle. When that cloth is worn, it means there has been no conception in the womb and no forthcoming birth to be expected. Nicodemus was a very self-righteous man, but Jesus informed him that he must be born again. There had been no conception in his heart by the Holy Spirit, and he had experienced no spiritual birth.

Before salvation we were dressed in the filthy rags of sin, but when we received Jesus as Savior, He dressed us in His own righteousness. We are now clothed in the righteousness of Jesus Christ. He took all our sin and gave us all His righteousness. Unto Him be glory! The old hymn, *The Solid Rock*, said it perfectly:

> *When He shall come with trumpet sound,*
> *Oh, may I then in Him be found;*
> *Dressed in His righteousness alone,*
> *Faultless to stand before the throne.*

We are Upright in Heart

The third descriptive phrase found in Psalm 32:11, revealing the identity of a Christian, is "upright in heart." Upright means "straight." A Christian is a person with a straight heart. Now that is not the heart

105

you had when you were born into this world. God described that heart in Jeremiah 17:9, *"The heart is deceitful above all things, and desperately wicked: and who can know it?"* The word "deceitful" means "crooked, twisted, polluted and perverted." That is the heart you possessed when you were born. The expression "desperately wicked" means that the original condition of the heart would have never gotten any better on its own. It was incurably diseased and could not have healed itself.

When Jesus came into your life, He did not slap a band aid on that old crooked, twisted, polluted, perverted heart. The Great Physician performed major surgery and gave you a new heart. You are not the person you used to be. You have been born again and recreated in the image of Jesus Christ. Unto Him be Glory!

II. WHAT WE ARE SUPPOSED TO BE DOING AS CHRISTIANS

Now that you know who you are, what are you supposed to be doing as a child of God? Psalm 32:11, gives us three specific exhortations.

Be Glad

First, we are to "be glad." The basic idea is to be full of cheer. I know a lot of Christians who need to cheer up, lighten up, and brighten up. There is no reason for a believer in Jesus to walk around in the doldrums of gloom and doom.

Dr. Gray Allison was the founder and first President of Mid-America Baptist Theological Seminary in Memphis, Tennessee. No other man influenced my life more than he did. I heard him say one day in a classroom setting, "I am not always happy, but I am always full of joy." Wow! What a terrific attitude for a Christian. Our happiness is based on externals which are constantly changing; but our joy, our cheerfulness, is based on an internal relationship with God, and He never changes, but is the same yesterday, today, and forever.

This idea of being glad involves making a choice. Do you know some people who are always down, always discouraged, always defeated? Do you know why they are like that? They choose to be like that. On the other hand, do you know some people who are always up, always positive in their outlook, always walking with a smile on their face? Do you know why they are like that? They choose to be like that.

As a child of God, you are in the Lord. You are a new creation. You will never face the condemnation of God, and you will never be separated from His love. Be glad, be full of cheer. Choose to be so full of gladness that it will overflow and bless the lives of others.

Rejoice

Next, the Psalmist exhorts us to rejoice. The word "rejoice" is an interesting word. It is not a noun. It is a verb. It is not a passive verb, however, it is an active verb. It literally means to turn around or spin about. It is a picture of dancing. It is not talking about that belly-rubbing stuff you did at your senior prom. It is talking about dancing in your heart before the Lord. 2 Samuel 6:14 says, *"And David danced before the LORD with all his might."* Why should David be the only believer to dance? The Word says, "rejoice, ye righteous." Those who are robed in righteousness are to rejoice. I used to be clothed in the filthy garments of sin, wickedness and ungodliness, but now I wear the kingly robes of righteousness and forgiveness. That makes me want to dance!

Shout for Joy

Finally, we are instructed to shout for joy. You can almost forget that in today's culture. People shout at sporting events and festive occasions, but hardly ever about spiritual things. I started preaching when I was sixteen years old. Back in those days many churches had youth-led revival meetings. I preached in lots of them as a teenager. I always loved preaching in the state of Mississippi. Back then, in almost every church in Mississippi where I preached, people would shout. They were not putting on a show or trying to draw attention to themselves. They were just so full of Jesus they either had to shout or explode. Not long ago I preached three back-to-back revival meetings in churches in Mississippi, and there was not one shout. They have gotten just as backslidden as churches in Alabama, Tennessee, Georgia and North Carolina (I am kidding . . . sort of).

We are to shout for joy. When God saved you, He filled your heart with joy. He did not fill you with joy just to make you feel good. His desire is for that inward joy to become an outward blessing that will benefit others. Do you know certain people that you just love to be around, to hang out with? Those are the people who bless you, encourage you, lift you up and even make you want to laugh. They are allowing their inward joy to be manifested in an outward expression in order to bless you and others like you.

You may be saying, "I could never shout." Okay, this may help. The word shout also means to sing aloud. Did you ever attend Vacation Bible School as a child? Do you remember singing a little song that said, *I've got the joy, joy, joy, joy down in my heart; down in my heart; down in my heart.* You were singing the joy on the inside to the outside. It needs to come out, has to come out, or it will die on the inside. Hey, you can never exhaust the supply. The more joy you dispense the more God will put in your heart.

"Well preacher, I cannot shout, and I cannot sing, so what do I do?" My friend, if you cannot shout or sing, then TALK it out. We live in an ever-talking society. We have lots of twenty-four-hour news channels on television, and all they do is talk, talk, talk. People talk about everything today. They talk about sports, food, aches and pains, and even the weather. Vance Havner used to quip:

Whether the weather be cold or

> *Whether the weather be hot,*
> *Whether the weather be good,*
> *or whether the weather be not;*
> *Whatever the weather,*
> *We'll weather the weather,*
> *Whether we like it or not.*

As Christians, it should be very natural for us talk about Jesus and what He has done in our lives. We used to be lost, but now we are found. We used to be on the way to Hell, but now we are Heaven bound. People speak about 7000 words a day. Let some of them be about Jesus. Shout it, sing it, or talk it; just DO it!

In closing, allow me to make an observation. As an itinerant evangelist, traveling from place to place, church to church, week after week, I do not see a lot of folks who are overflowing with cheer, dancing in their hearts before the Lord and shouting for joy. I can only conclude that joy-robbers have found a lodging place in many of our churches. Christians can never lose their salvation, but they can certainly lose their joy.

III. WHAT ROBS A CHRISTIAN OF JOY

Let me identify three major joy robbers that can be devastating to your Christian life.

Sin is a Joy Robber

When God saved you, He changed your disposition toward sin. Christians are not sinless, but God made it impossible for a believer to dabble around

110

in sin and be full of joy at the same time. Sin robs the child of God of his joy. I am not talking about what some describe as big sins.

A Christian does not go to bed one night in love with Jesus and wake up the next day and commit adultery. That does not happen. The follower of Jesus does not go to bed one night filled with the Holy Spirit and wake up the next morning and rob a bank. That just does not happen. Solomon said it is the little foxes that spoil the vine. Those so-called "little sins," often overlooked, can steal your joy. Such things as greed, jealousy, grudge-bearing, and gossiping are little foxes that can spoil the joy-producing vine in your life.

Critical, Negative Church Members are Joy Robbers

It seems that in many churches there are always a few people that are just plain troublemakers. Nothing ever goes to please them. They are always critical and negative concerning every issue that comes up. They are constantly causing division and seeking to enlist people to their side. One of the sternest verses in the New Testament declares, *"Now I beseech you, brethren, mark them which cause divisions and offences contrary to the doctrine which ye have learned, and avoid them"* (Romans 16:17). Paul says to mark them (be on guard against them) and avoid them (go out of your way to avoid them). Why? Because those people possess a very contagious spirit, and if you are not careful, you, too, will become like them. Remember, mark, and avoid.

111

Satan is a Joy Robber

Satan is miserable, and he desires that everyone else be miserable as well. He knows that he can never recapture the soul of a born-again believer, but he also knows he can rob them of their joy. He accomplishes that feat in two ways. First, he attempts to make believers doubt their salvation. The greatest thing on earth is to be saved, and the second greatest thing on earth is to know that you are saved. If the devil can get you to doubt your salvation, you will never be much of a witness for Christ. You will never have an effective prayer life, and you will never have real joy.

Second, the devil robs Christians of their joy by getting them to question the love of God. He delights in telling people that God does not love them or care anything about them. He whispers to the bereaved widow, "God doesn't love you. If God loved you, your husband would not be in the cemetery." He says to a broken-hearted mother and father, "God doesn't love you. If God loved you, your child would not have died in that automobile accident." If Satan can get you to doubt the love of God, your joy will be gone.

How is it with you? Have you allowed your joy to be stolen away? Are you constantly battling discouragement and sadness? If so, you need a personal revival. The greatest by-product of revival is a fresh baptism of joy. David begged the Lord, *"Wilt thou not revive us again: that thy people may rejoice in thee?"* (Psalm 85:6). If your joy is gone, get into the presence

112

of the Lord, confess every sin the Holy Spirit convicts you of, and ask God to revive your life, fill you with the Holy Spirit and restore your joy. He will. Yes, He will. Then be glad, rejoice and shout for joy. If you are not sure what to shout, try "UNTO HIM BE GLORY!"

Unto Him Be Glory

Made in the USA
Monee, IL
08 July 2023